Your Pastor: Preyed On or Prayed For?

How YOUR Church Can Do Incredible Things When YOU Pray for YOUR Pastor!

by

TERRY TEYKL

*"Write down the revelation and make
it plain on tablets so that a
herald may run with it."*

Habakkuk 2:2

YOUR PASTOR: PREYED ON OR PRAYED FOR?

Copyright © 1997 by Terry Teykl

First edition, April 1994
Second printing, August 1996
Second edition, September 1997
Fourth printing, August 1998

Unless otherwise indicated, all Scripture quotations are from the *Holy Bible, New International Version* © 1973, 1978, 1984 by the International Bible Society. Used by permission of Zondervan Publishing House.

ISBN: 1-57892-044-2

Printed in the United States of America.

Prayer Point Press
2100 N. Carrolton Dr. * Muncie, Indiana 47304
Phone: 765 759-0215
To order, call toll free: 1 (888) 656-6067

*This book is dedicated
to my wife, Kay, who
always saw to it that
I was prayed for.*

Contents

Preface

What a rare blessing it is indeed when God raises up a prophetic voice to speak with surgical precision to a specific need in the body. The need—the prayer of the saints for a beleaguered modern clergy facing unprecedented satanic assault.

The voice is Dr. Terry Teykl. Dr. Teykl has grasped the unique character of this attack as few have and with empathetic poignancy calls the house to order. It is high time we heed this appeal for effectual prayer protection for contemporary ministers. The scandal-ridden, demoralized, discouraged and disheartened ranks of western clergymen are sad testimony of prayerless churches who virtually invite demonic attack on their pastors.

This is not merely some dismal, diagnostic report, however, but an insightful blueprint for action. This book places within reach of the concerned a plan of action to meet headlong, in the power of the Spirit, a clear and present danger.

—*Mark Rutland, Pastor*
Calvary Assembly

Seven Ways this Book Can Help You and Your Church

Your Pastor: Preyed On or Prayed For? has been written to:

1. give you an inside look into your pastor's heart and mind and the seven areas where your help is needed most.

2. tell you how to begin, on your own, to use intercessory prayer to strengthen your pastor and his or her work.

3. show you step by step how you can become a spark plug to recruit other laypersons to pray for your pastor.

4. share easy-to-use ideas that will keep your prayer partners motivated and on track.

5. offer you specific prayers to use as models when you pray—prayers that address the seven unique needs of your pastor.

6. give you a checklist of 50 tested, proven ways to encourage laypersons to pray for their pastor.

7. describe strategies for minimizing destructive gossip about your pastor and bringing unity to your entire church.

From Funeral Home Chairs and Cereal Bowl Collection Plates to the Present

In 1968, U.S. combat forces in Vietnam had swelled to a half-million. The USS Pueblo was seized by North Korea. The Rev. Martin Luther King, Jr., and Senator Robert Kennedy were murdered. Richard Nixon was elected President. In Uppsala, Sweden, Protestant and Orthodox leaders from 80 countries met for the fourth annual assembly of the World Council of Churches.

On a personal note, 1968 was also the year I began my pastoral ministry by accepting a small rural appointment in east Texas.

Was I ever green! Fresh out of paganism, I had never taught a Sunday School class or preached a sermon.

During the first day of my new duties, I received a friendly phone call from a layman who asked, "Pastor Teykl, would you be willing to give the invocation at the high school assembly next Friday?"

I paused a moment before saying, "Sure, I'll be glad to."

After hanging up, and with great embarrassment, I reached for a dictionary to look up the meaning of "invocation."

How much progress I made in the following eleven years of pastoring churches in east and central Texas is still a matter of debate. Then in 1972, I had a "face-to-face" experience with the Holy Spirit that forever changed my life and the direction of my ministry.

Following that experience, in my unabated zeal and excitement to do God's work I offended nearly every person in our congregation. When the dust settled, only 20 of our little church's 100 members were still attending!

Believe me, I have written this book from personal experience. I know the pain of trying to be on the cutting edge of ministry and then being pushed over the edge by people who preferred the status quo over any kind of change.

Our entire family has suffered through my learning experiences. We know how stressful it is to live in someone else's home. My stomach got tied in knots and my wife cried when one of our four children burned a hole in the parsonage's new carpet. We've hung on with no money for groceries, no savings account, and a burden of debt that kept us from having any sense of financial security. To be candid, the *only* way I was able to stay on the road to seminary was by being a shade tree mechanic. I overhauled motors in order to make ends meet, and my wife pinched pennies until they hollered. The good news is that every member of our family came to know and deeply appreciate the abundant provisions of our heavenly Father.

I felt it was miraculous that I was able to attend Perkins School of Theology at Southern Methodist University. However, looking back, it was even more miraculous that I graduated with my core beliefs intact. Perkins is one of this country's most liberal seminaries. Their "biblical scholars" tried to convince me that the Holy Bible was a book of questionable reliability. I was shocked when I was told that Jesus was not born of a virgin, and that he was not raised from the dead. One seminarian summed up the philosophy of Perkins by saying, "Faith is believing in something you know ain't true!"

You can imagine how hurt, confused and angry I became when many of my most cherished beliefs were attacked. Yet, through the grace of God, I gained a deeper conviction that Jesus Christ is who he said he is. I know that he is the Savior of the world, and I believe with all my heart that the Bible is the Word of God.

In 1989, I was led to start a new church in College Station, Texas. When I arrived at my new assignment, I was greeted by eight members, no place to worship, no hymnals, no guaranteed salary and no budget. What's more, our "church" was $300,000 in debt!

Thank heavens, a local businessman donated 30 decrepit, wooden (and very uncomfortable) funeral home chairs. My wife, Kay, contributed two cereal bowls from our meager belongings to use as offertory plates. I'll be the first to admit that this beginning was austere, but it soon became clear that the future of Aldersgate United Methodist Church was truly blessed by the Holy Spirit.

A friend arranged for our first worship services to be held in the recreation room of a nearby apartment complex. Three months later, we moved to the Jewish synagogue. I felt like the Apostle Paul when I baptized our first convert in the synagogue.

Blessings of a Shoestring Beginning

The challenge to serve God had never been greater! Here I was, in the shadow of the mighty Texas A&M University, a rural preacher who had been called to start a new church in a community overflowing with PhDs. It was a humbling experience. Think about it: no office, telephone or computer. Not even a piano. Can you understand why I felt like a pastor in the Book of Acts?

Looking back, I am thankful because this shoestring beginning led me to discover the power of prayer in evangelism and in planting a new church. Through thick and thin, we remained faithful to our goal of building a Bible-based community of believers led by the Holy Spirit. We wanted to be on the cutting edge of renewal in worship, evangelism, cell groups, music and lay ministry. Our commitment was to stay in touch with the traditions of our faith. We felt that God had called us to witness to our denomination that we could build a great church by being positive and inclusive. That's why it was imperative for us to blend the old and the new to achieve a balanced expression of the Christian faith in our community.

From the start, prayer became the focal point of our efforts to reach College Station, Texas for Jesus Christ.

The Lord blessed us in ways most folks never dreamed possible. We launched our prayer ministry with 100 persons in January 1980. I didn't have to run any full-page ads in the *Dallas Morning News* or any spots on TV to let people know where they could find a place to join with others in opening their hearts to the Lord. Our efforts were blessed by Jesus Christ, and word of mouth was all the advertising we needed. People were drawn to our gatherings because they wanted to experience Jesus Christ and to become active members of our community of believers.

We met in homes, selected leaders, prayed and planned. Soon people were describing our meetings as "exciting."

Our little group quickly outgrew every building in which we worshiped. As if by some divine decree, the people who prayed with us began to think of themselves as part of a "church." Our services became more and more dramatic. Many accepted Jesus Christ as their Lord and Savior. Others reunited with the Holy Spirit. We prayed. They came. They stayed. And they invited their friends to join them in worship.

During the past 10 years, our church has welcomed 30,000 first time visitors. We have grown to an average attendance of 1,200 on Sunday mornings. These fine people don't just open their hearts to the Lord, they also open their pocketbooks to the poor. They have given over $1 million to feed, clothe and care for the less fortunate members of our community.

You know what I find most interesting? People who don't know the facts about our church and how we struggled to stand fast to our beliefs, raise money, select a site, build a building and hire a staff think they can explain how we got where we are today with one word: "luck." They think we grew dramatically because we "happened to be at the right place at the right time."

Fortunately, a lot of pastors and laypersons around the country realize we didn't get here by a stroke of fate. More often than not, these church leaders want to learn all they can about using prayer to strengthen their present churches—or to use prayer to plant new churches.

I receive hundreds of letters and phone calls each year that make the same request: "Tell us how you did it!"

You will recall that Jesus said, "It is written, . . . 'My house will be called a house of prayer,' " (Matthew 21:13). I use that verse of scripture as my mandate for action.

In 1984, I answered God's call to launch a renewal ministry to help pastors and their churches. The thesis guiding this ministry is simple. I encourage churches to emphasize prayer as much as they do Sunday School or annual pledge campaigns—in other words, to make prayer a top priority in the life of their churches. I highly recommend they focus their prayers on winning lost souls.

I suggest that churches select a prayer coordinator, choose a prayer format, recruit and train intercessors, take good care of them, give them feedback, build a prayer room and find creative ways to communicate with and serve God through prayer. I promise that when their churches pray they will experience the renewing power of the Holy Spirit in every department—and that they will win lost souls. As pastors and laypersons are touched by the Holy Spirit, they can evangelize their cities.

This book will make you aware of how many of today's best pastors are burned out, hurt and depressed. A surprising number haven't witnessed a profession of faith in years. I vividly remember a seminar in Vermont where a pastor raised his hand and asked, "What is a profession of faith? I haven't seen a conversion in so long that I really can't recall what one looks like!"

Don't be surprised to learn that a lot of pastors have "secret sins" and addictions that cause them to feel they are being held for ransom. A number of pastors' wives have cried openly as they relate how lonely and rejected they feel about being on the outside—unable to influence their families' lives. They and their children are being left with emotional scars that may never heal.

It's likely your pastor prays for every person in the church, yet he or she is probably the person least prayed for in your church!

Who prays for *your* pastor?

In 1986, my wife and I were asked to lead a revival at a large church in the Great Lakes region. The pastor is one of the most respected members of our denomination. To our dismay, he and his wife were "on medication" to deal with their serious depression. To say that his church was suffering from a crisis in leadership is an understatement. It was obvious that this once faithful servant had fallen on hard times and urgently needed the prayers of his entire membership. An abundance of people there wanted me to know their pastor had fallen from grace. However, not one person said he or she was praying that the pastor would overcome his problems and regain his position of leadership.

On Sunday, my wife used Ephesians 6 to teach a class on spiritual warfare. Her message became a turning point for all of us. As she spoke, the Lord gave me the outline of a guide that laypersons could use to pray for their pastors. The easy-to-understand guide proved to be a remarkably effective tool for helping laypersons to pray for their pastors. It offers a way for individuals like yourselves to place the full armor of God on the seven most critical areas of a pastor's life. This is what we call "hedging in" the pastor. [*Editor's note:* The image of a protective hedge comes from Job 1:10 where Satan accuses God of protecting Job from evil by putting "a hedge around him and his household . . ."]

You will find this Prayer Guide on page 57 and 58 of the manual *Preyed On or Prayed For.* You have my permission to reproduce these two pages and distribute them to the members of your local church who share your need for praying for your pastor. I hope that every member of your church will want one, and that they will keep this prayer guide in their Bibles.

When news of the prayer guide spread, thousands of pastors and laypersons from across the church wrote or called to request copies. Their response was almost overwhelming. It told me that we had touched a nerve close to the heart of what was troubling churches across America.

The demand for me to teach workshops on praying for pastors grew beyond all expectations. Soon I was not able to fill all of the requests. People in nearly every state were asking me to write a book that would help them strengthen their churches by mobilizing laypersons to pray for their pastors.

Feet of Clay

Before you read any further, there is one thing I want to confess. I, too, have feet of clay.

In 1987, I went through a personal crisis and burnout. The needs of my rapidly growing church and my attempt to fulfill all of the requests to lead workshops got out of hand. I tried to live up to the expectations of everyone who asked me for help. There simply weren't enough hours in the day. At the time, I was a devout codependent who was committed to a ministerial model of rugged individualism. One year I was away from home 80 days trying to handle other people's problems. I couldn't say "No."

Back home in College Station, the staff of my church endured a number of crises that were a direct result of my absence from leadership. I crashed and burned because my spiritual pantry was bare. With the encouragement of my wife and children, and at the insistence of my official board, I took time off and went for counseling.

You remember the story of how the cobbler's kids had no shoes? Well, because I was laboring under an image of total self-sufficiency, I had been remiss in asking members of my own church to pray for me!

When I finally admitted my human frailties by stating from the pulpit that I had a serious problem and that I needed the prayers of *every* member of my church, my life took a dramatic turn for the better. People began praying and I entered into an entirely new relationship with my flock. I would not have remained in ministry without the prayers of these saints.

Prayer won the day for me—and gave me back my life. I am most grateful for each layperson who has ever prayed for me. Only through their spiritual support has my ministry been able to endure its darkest days. When a layperson told me that he or she was praying for me, I felt sustained. When I was ready to throw in the towel, it was the prayers of the members of my church, my parents, my wife and my children that meant everything to me. They made the difference. I came to realize that we have all fallen from grace and we are all members of the same team.

A great writer once told me that "being subtle is to risk not making the point." That is why I write the way I think—plainspoken and from the heart.

This book is written for laypersons who genuinely love their shepherds and want to learn how to better support them through prayer. Right now, my prayer is that the simple plan outlined on the following pages will enable you to become the spark plug that ignites the interest of others in your church to start praying for your pastor.

Today, my life, my ministry and my church are a living testimony to the power of prayer and what it can do for *your* church!

Chapter One

Meet Your Own Pastor: The Inside Story

You've probably wondered what your pastor is *really* like.

Naturally, we pastors are all unique. The range of our personalities, philosophies and theologies is as diverse as in the rest of the human race. We have a tendency to be guarded in areas where we feel most vulnerable. Because most of us are reluctant to lower our defenses, a lot of people think we don't live in the "real world."

Remember the movies of the 1950s and 1960s that showed a priest who got so mad he said something "secular," or took a punch at the villain? You could almost hear the audience cheer!

As a layperson, your mental image of your pastor is probably one of preaching, baptizing, conducting weddings, counseling couples and performing other duties required to fulfill his or her vows. It's likely you don't think about your pastor balancing a personal checking account, disciplining off-spring, pressing a suit, hunting like crazy for something he or she misplaced—or taking a day off to pursue a favorite hobby.

> *Your pastor has a personality that is played out behind the closed doors of the parsonage.*

Although hundreds of pastors have shared with me the pains, aspirations, shortcomings and accomplishments of their private lives, I can't tell you what happens when *your* minister is not ministering. All I can hope is that you will be aware that your pastor has a personality that is played out behind the closed doors of the parsonage.

I *can* share with you six key things that all of the pastors I have come to know on a personal basis have in common.

Six Things All Pastors Have in Common

1. A CALL TO MINISTRY

John Wesley felt his heart "strangely warmed," and knew immediately that God had chosen him. A young man from Georgia related how, while walking in the woods, whistling the tune to "What A Friend We Have In Jesus," he felt "called." A college student from Seattle told about being visited by the Holy Spirit in a dream. "I awakened and sat up in bed," she said. "The entire room was filled with a presence I had never before known. I knew in my heart that God was calling me to lead others to the light." Ask any pastor about the call to ministry, and you will hear about one of the most inspiring experiences of his or her life.

2. HIGH MOMENTS OF AFFIRMATION

Every pastor has "mountaintop" experiences that become the highlights of his or her ministry. Many would agree it includes those times when entire families join the church, or when a hardened sinner steps forward to accept Jesus Christ as Lord and Savior. For Billy Graham, it's probably the sight of a hundred thousand or more people who have filled a stadium to hear him deliver the Word of God. Regardless of the level of affirmation, it's the moment when a pastor feels that the wind is blowing the right way. God is present. The pastor has a sensation of soaring on wings like eagles, running and not growing weary, walking and not fainting.

Personally, I know of no other calling that offers even close to the sheer joy and fulfillment of pastoring a local church. Every time I baptize a child, unite couples in holy matrimony or place my arm around the shoulder of a convert to the Christian faith, I get a lump in my throat and goose bumps up and down my arms. These are events of unprecedented significance in my life, and they affirm my commitment to serve God to the very best of my abilities.

3. LOW MOMENTS OF FRUSTRATION

Maybe it's something simple—like the times I had to choose between taking one of my children to a special event at school or counseling a couple whose marriage unexpectedly headed for the rocks. Or, it can be more complicated and have far greater consequences.

For example, a pastor from Kansas cut short his long-overdue vacation and drove all night to get home in time to conduct the funeral of one of his dearest members.

The family sat quietly until, during the eulogy, he announced with unbridled admiration that the deceased had left her entire estate to his church. Relatives seated in the family section were visibly shaken and many began to cry in a way that surpassed normal expressions of grief at the loss of a loved one. Their tears quickly turned to anger.

As the pall bearers were carrying the casket out of the church, the pastor heard the deceased woman's son tell his sister that they had been "done in" by the pastor. Later, as the son walked away from the graveside ceremony, he turned to the pastor and, with tears streaming down his face and a stony chill in his voice, said, "I'll see you in court, preacher!"

The following week, the pastor received notification from another church in his city that six of his most loyal members had transferred their memberships to a sister denomination.

4. THE FEAR OF FAILURE

Do you prefer to think of your pastor as being super human? Most people do. Yet, recently the pastor of one of America's largest churches told me, "My greatest fear is the fear of failing." He is expected to exude confidence every Sunday morning to a gathering of 5,000 people who want to hear the Word of God. But inside, his fear of failing is destroying his own self-confidence!

In spite of the burden I carry to be bold in preaching accountability to sinners, I would be less than honest if I said I didn't tone down my message because I feared alienating some of my members whose support I felt was vital to our mission. While it's popular for us to criticize "glib-tongued politicians" who water down their every comment to avoid offending any constituents, I've heard a number of pastors admit they are afraid to hold people's feet to the fire. As one observer said, "It's not a good idea for a pastor to get too close to the fire. *He* might get burned!"

It's not just preaching that can get the clergy in trouble. The wife of a prominent Chicago business executive turned to her pastor for guidance on how to break off an affair she was having with one of her husband's partners. That evening over dinner, the pastor confided to his wife the name and circumstances of the member who was engaged in the adulterous relationship. The pastor's wife let details of the affair "slip" to an old classmate who happened to call from San Francisco. The news quickly ricocheted back to the husband in Chicago. By noon of the following day, the pastor's credibility as a counselor was devastated.

"I'm afraid to confide anything to my wife," he said. "And she is the *only* person with whom I felt I could tell my innermost secrets."

As sad as it may sound, every pastor I have met has hidden fears—not the least of which is the fear of failure.

5. AT LEAST A TINGE OF SPIRITUAL MELT-DOWN

The pastor of one of the West Coast's largest independent churches has every right to be proud. He built his thriving congregation of more than 10,000 members from scratch, going door to door to invite them to join the new community church he was organizing. His charisma and sincerity got people in the door, and his preaching led them to pack the pews on Sunday morning. Today, the church might best be described as an oasis for its members. From fancy swimming pools and workout rooms to bowling alleys and social centers, the church offers all the amenities of a well-financed country club.

The problem is, after spending a quarter of a century and a lot of hard work in building this impressive edifice, the pastor has let the good life lead him down the path to spiritual meltdown. He is presently "seeing" his young secretary. The pastor's wife has become a closet alcoholic. When they are not at each other's throats, they are giving each other the silent treatment. Today, the only thing they enjoy doing together is going to the race track and betting money that has been siphoned off from Sunday's offerings.

When members ask to see their pastor to discuss personal problems, they are quickly and diplomatically referred to one of the ministers who has been trained in counseling. "I don't deal with people's personal problems," the pastor says. "That's for my staff."

In spite of the fact his members think he is an organizational genius, and they love his fine sermons, the pastor is spiritually dead.

Be assured, his "death" did not occur overnight. It started when, according to his wife, he "eased off" on praying for the individual needs of his flock. Later, he started having an occasional glass of wine with dinner. That lead to "sampling" other alcoholic beverages. A short time later, a member who wanted the pastor to sanctify his gambling invited the minister to sit in his box seat and "watch the ponies race around the track." With a little encouragement, the pastor agreed to let his friend make a $2 bet on his behalf. The rest is history.

Of course, it's easy for a pastor in College Station (with no racetrack) to condemn a fellow pastor thousands of miles away. But I don't know all that many pastors who feel they are holding the line on moral issues. From what I have witnessed, "social drinking" is clearly rampant among pastors in a number of denominations. According to a nationwide survey, 18 percent are hooked on pornography and 37 percent have been involved in what they describe as "inappropriate sexual behavior" with someone in their church. Some 80 percent believe their ministry is affecting their families negatively. Do you detect a "tinge" of spiritual meltdown among the ranks of some of our most respected pastors?

6. THE NEED FOR SPIRITUAL SUPPORT FROM LAYPERSONS

A middle-aged man, the graduate of one of this country's most renowned schools of divinity, recently left the pastoral ministry to sell life insurance.

"I had a rough time dealing with all of our members' expectations," he said, "but it never dawned on me to ask for the prayers of our members." For years, all of his attention was focused on his members and *their* needs. "Last year, my wife left me to start a life of her own," he said. "She's bitter about the church and what it took from us. Believe me, I loved my wife very much. Our marriage simply couldn't take the stress of being a pastor 24 hours a day, seven days a week. No one but a pastor knows the burden of my being a shepherd. Pastors urgently need the prayers of their laity in order to survive."

Another pastor said that parishioners are not hesitant in asking him to pray for *their* needs. "A layperson has never offered to pray for me and my needs," he said. "I wouldn't know where to begin!"

It should come as no surprise that, at some time during their ministry, most pastors have seriously considered seeking employment in a secular profession. The headquarters of one of the largest denominations in the United States has letters of resignation and dismissal stacked "knee deep." Wouldn't it be better to mobilize a prayer force to *retain* our best pastors rather than to encourage their resignations by our neglect?

I hope you will take a moment before you turn the page to reflect on the insights you have gained from reading this first chapter. Because you are reading this book, I know that you care greatly about your pastor and his or her ministry. Right now, until you can recruit other laypersons to help, the future of your pastor's ministry may well rest in *your* hands.

Chapter Two

Is Your Pastor Preyed On, or Prayed For?

"Minister Resigns Over Misconduct 'Long Ago.'"

That bold headline stared at Nashville's Rev. David Maynard from the front page of the November 23, 1993 edition of *The Tennessean*. It had to be one of the most heartbreaking moments of his life.

One of the city's highest profile pastors was being asked to resign from his once-thriving church. The action was taken following allegations that he had an affair five years before with a woman he was counseling, and had been involved in four other affairs earlier in his ministry.

A laywoman said the 350-member church has become "painfully divided" over the issue. "It's split the church," she explains.

"His supporters want to fight his firing," a former parishioner reported. "They believe

Maynard is the victim of a small group of religious zealots who are incapable of forgiving his previous indiscretions." Whether or not Maynard is the victim of a "witch hunt," as one member called the probe, is still being debated.

Those who want the minister terminated immediately point to the 30 to 50 members who have stopped worshiping because of the turmoil. "The trust has been broken," an opponent of the pastor said. "He's got to go!"

This isn't an isolated incident . . .

A recent study, "Sexual Harassment in the United Methodist Church," revealed that of the nearly 600 individuals surveyed, 23 percent of the laywomen said they had been harassed, 17 percent by their own pastor and 9 percent by another pastor. An earlier report by the ecumenical Washington Association of Churches concluded that "sexual abuse on the part of the pastor and pastoral counselors is more widespread than commonly believed."

I believe that Satan hates pastors.

I believe that Satan hates pastors.

Last week, a pastor from Maine called me to confess adultery. On Monday, one of Oklahoma's promising young pastors informed me that he has AIDS. Tuesday afternoon, a newly married pastor from Indiana told me his bride has admitted that she is a lesbian. Thursday, I received a letter from a pastor whose admission of sin made me cry. And on Friday, I opened the newspaper to find an article about a priest from Chicago who is being charged with molesting more than a dozen young boys.

Is it any wonder that laypersons are confused?

The retired pastor of a suburban Kansas City church professed that, "All pastors have their human frailties. Some have problems with alcohol, others seem to attract women like magnets. And there are those who blatantly plagiarize other preachers' sermons so they can slip away for golf or worse. I've never met a pastor who wasn't having a problem in some area of his life."

A friend recently commented that "modern pastorates look like the road from Kuwait to Baghdad after the Gulf War—burned out and abandoned."

My contacts within the church lead me to believe that a growing number of pastors feel used and blown to bits—men and women who may never preach with fire and boldness again. Some can be piled together as moral failures, unable to move because they are bogged down in guilt and shame. Others feel lost with no direction and a deep sense of fear. Many are troubled by a loss of identity. They lack the confidence to move in any direction. It's a pitiful sight.

Pastors who once preached with passion have surrendered to the forces of evil and now, herding with others who have fallen from grace, often lament their problems and talk with disdain about fellow pastors who have not erred—or have not been caught in their indiscretions.

Why is the highway littered with defeat and spiritual death? Could it be that we take our pastors for granted and *shoot* them instead of praying for them?

If this is the case, I wonder if it is too late for us to repent for our lack of prayer for our shepherds and bear the fruit of repentance in a new zeal to pray for them.

Modern pastors are not the first to come under attack. Biblical pastors had their share of struggles also. In Exodus 17, Pastor Moses is having a hard time. At Rephidim, the Israelites are short on water and they blame Moses, their pastor! The people call a meeting of the B.T.E. (Back to Egypt) Committee to grumble against Moses. When he hears about their meeting, Moses is frustrated, and asks the Lord, "What am I to do with these people? They are almost ready to stone me." So the Lord comes to his rescue, provides water, and the B.T.E Committee adjourns.

Moses probably thought his troubles were over. But just as everyone settles down, the Amalekites attack. Pastor Moses orders Joshua into battle and takes Aaron and Hur to the top of the hill to pray. As Moses watches the battle, he lifts his hands over the people. We read that

> As long as Moses held up his hands, the Israelites were winning, but whenever he lowered his hands, the Amalekites were winning.

As the battle continues, Aaron and Hur notice that Moses' hands are growing tired, and they quickly discern the danger this might cause the Israelites. So Aaron and Hur took a stone, sat their pastor on it between them, and held up his weary hands. Verse 12 says that Moses' hands "remained steady till sunset." The end result was a victory for the people of God! What a beautiful demonstration of support for a tired, battle-worn pastor.

Who is holding up *your* pastor's hands?

On one hand pastors need prayer protection for themselves and their families. We are battling the enemy who comes "only to steal and kill and destroy" (John 10:10). He preys on pastors with an arsenal of destructive forces. On the other hand, since pastors do spiritual work, they need prayer for spiritual anointing and blessing.

In your prayers, you can ask God to make your pastor fruitful. Jesus told his disciples in John 15:7-8, ". . . ask whatever you wish, and it will be given you. This is to my Father's glory, that you bear much fruit, . . ." The Holy Spirit honors prayers for pastors by blessing their work, both preaching and soul-winning. A prayed-for pastor is protected and blessed.

Ironically, sometimes the pastor is the least prayed for person in the local church. He or she may live in a nice house and receive good pay, yet be neglected in the prayers of the flock. This can happen for several reasons. For example, with so many other prayer needs in the church, the pastor may feel too embarrassed to ask for prayer. Perhaps everyone views the pastor as the one who should pray for the congregation's needs and the needs of the world, failing to realize that the pastor needs prayer, too.

Prayer support means more than just dashing off a few prayer phrases once in a while on the pastor's behalf. By prayer support, I am talking about a hedge of people recruited, planted, trained, aimed and motivated to consistently pray for the pastor.

As a layperson, you are responsible for making this happen, and this book can teach you how to do it. C. Peter Wagner is right when he notes in his book *Prayer Shield*,

> In a word—pastors need help—at least more help than they have been getting. In the course of a year, I meet and interact with hundreds of pastors. Even though I do not relate to them as a counselor or as pastor to pastor, I find that many are beaten up spiritually, emotionally, and sometimes physically.[1]

Seven Areas Where Your Pastor Comes Under Attack

"Some members may fall asleep when I'm preaching on Sunday morning, but you can bet they keep 'one eye open' to see how I live my life the rest of the week."

That's the sentiment of a minister who transgressed once too often and was caught. Now he feels the close scrutiny of his 1,250-member church in west Los Angeles. "Living the life of a pastor is a mine field," he said. "Ever since the Jimmy Swaggart and Jim Bakker scandals, every preacher in the country has ended up on someone's 'watch list.'"

Pastors need to be prayed for, not preyed on! My goal in this chapter is not to condemn pastors for the problems that haunt them. Rather, it is to provide you with a more in-depth look at the challenges pastors are facing—and to seek your prayers and blessings in helping ease or remove their burdens. During the many seminars I have conducted, it has been my privilege to meet and visit with thousands of pastors. Based on what they told me are their greatest needs, I want to help you understand where *they* feel your prayers can help them the most.

The seven areas in your pastor's life and ministry that are most likely to come under attack are his or her (1) private life, (2) family life, (3) praise life, (4) prayer life, (5) professional life, (6) preaching life and (7) persevering life.

Your Pastor's Private and Family Life

Meet Frank. He's ministering to the people served by a 3-point charge in rural New Mexico, and he is a *good* pastor. In order to remain readily available to his far-flung flock, Frank wears a beeper on his belt and carries a cellular phone in his attache. When he is not preaching a sermon, ministering to the sick, recruiting new members, handling the maintenance of his three churches or performing any of the 101 other duties of a pastor, Frank is riding in a patrol car talking to the officers he serves as police chaplain. Last month, he launched a 12-step recovery program for drug addicts.

What's the problem?

Big-hearted Frank has no life of his own. He is *always* on call. His private life is suffering, and his wife is hooked on over-the-counter medications for her frayed nerves. "I love Frank," she says, "but I hate the strain his duties are placing on our marriage. Even during our most intimate moments, I have to worry about the phone ringing or his beeper going off."

Frank and his wife aren't alone. At a small church in upstate New York, the pastor's wife is boiling mad about having to live in a parsonage with a side door that leads right into the church. "People treat our home like it is their church's fellowship hall," she says. "They think nothing of 'raiding' our kitchen for whatever supplies and utensils are needed for Wednesday night dinners."

To add insult to injury, the pastor's wife is expected to attend *all* of the women's functions. "When I'm five minutes late, someone sticks her head in our side door and hollers, 'Shirley, are you coming to our meeting?' What is expected of a pastor's wife is unreal."

Some 10 percent of all pastors admit their family life has "suffered greatly" as a result of their current ministry.

In a survey conducted by *Spice*, a newsletter for wives of ministers, one respondent wrote that "by the time my pastor-husband gets through unloading all of his own problems and the problems of his members on me, he's too tired to listen to *my* problems." Then, without signing her name, she added the following postscript: "I am having an affair with our organist. He's old enough to be my father, but at least he listens to me and makes me feel like *I* am the most important person in his life!"

Adults aren't the only ones who suffer. Children of pastors have a common complaint that the church *always* takes precedence over their needs. "My dad's a great guy," the daughter of a pastor in Salem, Oregon says. "I just wish he would give me some of the attention he gives his parishioners."

George Barna interviewed a 12-year veteran pastor who admitted, "Sometimes I feel ashamed to go to church on Sunday because of how our family is struggling."[2] When all hell is breaking loose in the parsonage, it's hard

> *"I just wish he would give me some of the attention he gives his parishioners."*

to stand up on Sunday morning and be full of the joy of the Lord.

Most people, even pastors, find work a difficult place to be when things aren't going well at home. It is easy to forget that pastors are only human, and that they also have to deal with all of the problems that go along with living in a fallen world. We are all vulnerable to personal attacks against ourselves and our families.

A recent survey revealed that 17 percent of the ministers in the United States are burned out. That is one in five. Pastors, believe it or not, get lonely because there are so few they can really share with about their private lives.

In addition to attacks from the outside, a pastor and his family may feel the sting of darts fired from within the church itself. One of the tragedies of the Gulf War was the accidental shooting of our own soldiers by our own guns. Today there is a similar tragedy that is deadly to a pastor's well-being: friendly fire in the church. When things go wrong in the church, the pastor gets the blame. Pastors come under friendly fire when they are criticized and accused by their own church members. Often, their spouses are directly wounded in the fire also, or indirectly wounded when pastors go home to unload on mates.

When accused or criticized, pastors will lose confidence and begin to retreat. One recent study showed that after ten years of ministry, 70 percent of pastors had lost their confidence. The boldness they need to proclaim the gospel is dulled by the fear of being shot by one of their own. A pastor cannot effectively fight the world while caught in the crossfire of church politics or factions.

It is almost impossible to take aim at someone you are earnestly lifting up in prayer. Therefore, the more people you recruit in your church to pray for your pastor, the fewer will be left to join the firing squad! Prayer hedges help create an atmosphere of appreciation and love for the pastor and his or her family, shielding them from friendly fire.

Your Pastor's Praise and Prayer Life

Say "hello" to Ray. He is the 27-year-old pastor of a historic little church in the southernmost foothills of the Appalachian mountains. After lunch last Saturday, Ray went to the community funeral home to comfort the family of one of his closest friends and his most outspoken supporter. For Ray, this church member's death was a very personal loss. As he embraced the widow and her two young sons to pray, tears streamed down his cheeks. The young pastor felt drained as he left the mourners behind and hurried to the nearest florist to pick up flowers he had ordered to decorate the church for a wedding that evening.

At 7:00 P.M., he stood in front of a deliriously happy couple and performed the wedding ceremony. Following the reception, Ray immediately went to his study. There he spent an hour polishing the sermon he would preach the following morning, and two hours preparing the eulogy he would deliver on Monday.

For Ray and other pastors, life is an emotional roller coaster. Because ministers are usually in contact with dozens of members every day of the week, they often confront disappointment, joy, grief, fear and most of the other human emotions that affect the people who seek out their pastors to celebrate the good times and help them get through the tough times.

That is why worship and praise are so important for pastors. Worship fills their cups, and praise revives them emotionally. Pastors thrive on good worship!

When does your pastor worship God? He or she is the *leader* of worship. Yet, when your pastor steps into the pulpit, a great deal more enters his or her mind than simply delivering the sermon.

Chances are, your pastor has to think about the thermostat, a shortage of workers in the nursery, spotting any special guests, remembering all of the announcements, and a lot of other non-worship concerns. Of course, in the midst of it all, your pastor is trying to stay tuned-in to the expressions on the faces of the worshipers and to what the Holy Spirit may be saying during the worship service.

Could it be that the pastor worships *less* than any other person at the service? If this is the case, your pastor's spiritual and emotional cup may not be getting filled. His or her hands may be growing weary and falling to the side. Depression and burnout often follow when

> *Could it be that the pastor worships less than any other person at the service?*

the pastor is deprived of good, intimate, exalted corporate and private worship.

How about your pastor's *prayer* life? Just as the emotional roller coaster may rob your pastor of good praise time, "busyness" can steal away the average pastor's prayer life.

According to a former pastor who is now president of a church college in Wisconsin, "A pastor lives in a 'pressure cooker' of unrealistic expectations." After pausing a moment, he adds, "Listen to what a pastor says when one of his members approaches him. The pastor will invariably feel compelled to say something to justify what he is doing at the moment. For example, if he is having lunch with a layman, and another church member comes over to their table, the pastor will say, 'Just having lunch with one of our finest members,' or something to that effect."

A pastor from Michigan agreed: "It's a sad commentary, but we pastors stay constantly busy trying to live up to someone else's expectations."

What do *pastors* think lay people expect of them? George Barna provides us the answer from his recent survey:

1. Live an exemplary life.
2. Be available at all times to all people for all purposes.
3. Lead the church to grow numerically.
4. Balance wisdom with leadership and love.
5. Teach people the deeper truths of the faith in ways that are readily applicable in all life situations.
6. Be committed to your family and demonstrate spiritual leadership in your family; love your spouse and provide a positive role model for children.
7. Keep pace with the latest trends and developments of church life.
8. Build significant relationships with members of the congregation.
9. Represent the church in the community.
10. Grow spiritually.
11. Run the church in a crisp, professional, businesslike manner without taking on a cold, calculating air.[3]

What time does that leave for a pastor to pray?

Most pastors desire stronger prayer lives, yet the average time spent in prayer among evangelical pastors according to one national poll is only seven minutes a day. C. Peter Wagner did a survey of 572 American pastors across regional, age and denominational lines. He found that 57 percent pray less than 20 minutes a day, 34 percent pray between 20 minutes and one hour a day, and 9 percent pray one hour or more a day. The average prayer time according to his survey was 22 minutes per day. He also found that 28 percent, or approximately 1 out of 4, pray less than 10 minutes a day![4]

The desire to pray is preyed on by church administration, budget matters, visitation, public relations, church maintenance, endless committee meetings and various practical services like giving Sister Jones a ride to church. Sometimes the telephone can become the worst enemy of a pastor's strong, consistent prayer life. Plus, pastors, like others, are subject to laziness, impatience, rebelliousness and unconfessed sin.

Yet, "busyness" is no new problem, for the early church also had to deal with overwhelming demands in its beginning. The first five chapters of Acts report an estimated 20,000 conversions! In Acts 6, the apostles elected deacons to wait on tables so they could devote themselves to prayer and the ministry of the Word. They knew how to delegate.

As you know, your pastor is a professional, but what he does is spiritual. He evangelizes the lost, teaches about God, prays for the sick and counsels the wounded. Since all ministry is rooted in the Holy Spirit, the pastor needs the Spirit's anointing to present Jesus with power and authority.

A pastor who takes the time to praise God and pray in the Holy Spirit is built up and blessed spiritually and emotionally. Jude writes, "But you, dear friends, build yourselves up in your most holy faith and pray in the Holy Spirit" (verse 20). On several occasions in Luke, when Jesus prayed, the Spirit came on him also. We read in Luke 3:21-22, ". . . as he was praying, heaven was opened and the Holy Spirit descended on him in bodily form like a dove." In Acts 2, while the apostles were praying continually, the Spirit came upon them as well. We receive the Holy Spirit when we pray, and more especially, the Spirit receives us.

Your pastor needs to be refreshed through prayer and praise daily, especially when he or she is being stretched beyond human limits to minister, counsel and care for the flock.

Your pastor needs *your* help!

One of the most critical elements of any successful ministry is the pastor's own spiritual life. A pastor who is too busy to spend time alone with God is headed for trouble. If the enemy can keep a pastor too burdened to make a joyful noise in praise, or keep that pastor out of the prayer closet, then he can cut the pastor off from the vital Source, and the anointing that pastor needs to present Jesus to the world.

Let's take a look at Pastor Caroline. She is a devoted pastor who rises early to pray, spending two hours each morning in prayer. She preaches on prayer and calls her church to pray for the lost. She is always looking for ways to bring her people to pray for their city to be taken for God. Because she truly desires to hear from God, one day a week she fasts for her seminar preparation.

Caroline's church is rapidly outgrowing its building, which seats 200, and so it is packed

for both worship services. Five to ten new families are visiting every week. As the church is
growing, hurting people are being attracted,
many of whom need or want to be counseled by
Caroline personally. She is doing more and more,
and staying up later and later to return phone
calls. She is finding it harder to get up in the
morning. In a growing church, everybody wants
something from her—her time, her prayer, her
presence or her advice.

Slowly, the demands of her growing church
begin to eat away at Caroline's two hour morning prayer sessions, and she finds herself praying less and less. Pastor Caroline's hands are not
as high as they used to be. And to add to her
growing frustration, she is plagued by the tyranny of the unfinished because every day more
and more is left undone.

The pressure on your pastor, as on Pastor
Caroline, can be unreal. Most believe it is a privilege to lead God's people into a deeper relationship with him. More frequently than not, however, the privilege fits around the pastor's neck
like a noose. "It's only by the grace of God," the
pastor reasons, "the slack in the rope has not
been tightened."[5]

As a layperson, you can stand in the gap for
your pastor's spiritual life to make sure that the
enemy does not rob him or her of vital worship
and prayer time. As believers, we all have authority and power in Jesus' name to stand against
any of the enemy's assignments, and to build up
a hedge of protection around those we pray for.

Does anyone in your church support your
pastor in this way, or is everyone too busy try-

ing to get what they can from the pastor? Do the deacons encourage your pastor to take time away and pray? Does your Board insist that your pastor take a week every year to go on a retreat to seek God?

Perhaps you can instigate some of these thoughts. Not only will your pastor be grateful and encouraged, but you will begin to see the results as the Spirit enables your pastor and fills his or her cup.

Your Pastor's Professional Life, Preaching Life and Persevering Life

Let me introduce you to Don. He is the pastor of a newly-constructed church on the outskirts of Jacksonville, Florida. The neighborhood is upper middle class. A number of homes have swimming pools and patios. Across the street from the church, a large apartment complex is nearing completion.

Last week, five of the church's leading laymen asked Don to join them for lunch. Halfway through the meal, the group's self-appointed spokesman cleared his throat and said, "Pastor, we are deeply concerned about our church's lack of growth. We know you had a vision, and you've tried a number of approaches. But, quite frankly, they aren't working. The Baptist church is growing by leaps and bounds, and our church isn't." Don shifted uneasily in his chair as the spokesman continued. "We love you, and we want the best for you. We told you that when we hired you. But, we've got to start thinking about what's best for our church."

Don's stomach was tied in knots as he drove home, deeply hurt and frustrated. *What should*

I do? he asked himself. *Should I go or stay? How can I tell my daughter that she may have to transfer during her senior year of high school? What will my wife say if she has to quit her job and pack up for another move? Lord, what am I to do?*

When things aren't going as expected in a church, usually the pastor gets blamed.

Satan can use well-meaning but insensitive people and the circumstances surrounding a pastor's life to try and throw him or her off the course that God has set. When a pastor wants to try something new, the old-timers often resist change by digging in their heels. For example, a pastor in Indiana told me about a lady in his church who would get up and walk out of the sanctuary the moment he started to preach. Resisting change provided her the attention she was looking for. In a church that I previously pastored, when I stepped into the pulpit, a woman who invariably sat in the front pew would place her fingers in her ears to avoid hearing me preach. That is persistent resistance!

Since the working life of your pastor is the most visible to the congregation and to his or her peers, it is often the most attacked area. The enemy can shoot darts at your pastor's professional life through other preachers or political forces. He can attack your pastor's preaching life through the flock itself or through factions in the church as he tries to wear down your pastor's persevering life as he or she strives to finish the race.

A pastor also may feel intimidated or frustrated by power groups in the church. It is amazing what a small group of four or five can do to a pastor's confidence. A man in a small town in Ohio appointed himself to his church's welcoming committee, and would greet visitors by asking them to go back to where they came from.

Quite often, your pastor's professional life can come under attack from all sides, and even your pastor's peers can be used as a force against him or her. Most pastors get saturated with ideas from successful pastors, creating "information overloads." Also, pastors can face political forces and competition within their denominations. Preachers' meetings can be depressing when the numbers game or salary ladder is the chief source of conversation.

Meet Pastor Chris. He loves to preach and considers this his highest calling as a pastor. He believes in the power of the spoken word to convict, convince and bring people to salvation, and he is deeply convinced that the Word of God inspires, rebukes, heals and conforms the church to the image of God in Jesus Christ. He seeks God for messages that speak to his

> *It is amazing what a small group of four or five can do to a pastor's confidence.*

church's heart, vision and mission. He also tries to interpret the times to his people when in the pulpit, so he wants to be prayed up and read up. As a shepherd, he tries to have a good feel of where his flock is. His church is over 3,000 in membership, with a staff of 16 full-time employees. During the week, he preaches four services in his downtown church, two on Sunday morning, one on Sunday night, and one on Wednesday night.

His sermons are good and practical, and people drive from the outskirts to hear him preach. Because of this, he wants to preach powerful and faithful messages each service, but he is hard-pressed for study time. Now in his thirteenth year, Chris is feeling pressured to come up with new material. He counsels the hurting, he administers the church, and he holds his staff intact and on course. Churches in his denomination are continually asking him to come and conduct preaching missions, and his board of deacons has voted to build a new church out in the growth area. Now there will be even more meetings. At home, his three children need his attention. Chris's problem is one of preparation. When can he find time to study and be prayed up? This pastor feels his hands growing tired.

According to Barna, just over 70 percent of the pastors he surveyed said that either preaching, teaching or discipling people is their primary source of joy in the ministry. But with all the other demands on their time, it is difficult for many to feel adequately prepared. He found that 77 percent of the senior pastors spend at least 6 hours per week preparing sermons, and many of those spend well over 10 hours. Barna states, "Ministry is tough work, and thousands of pastors bear the scars to prove it. Although many lay members idealize the work of the clergy, the harsh reality is that despite the best efforts of these learned individuals and regardless of the high and holy nature of the calling, pastoring a church is more burdensome than most people realize."[6]

Here is a frightening statistic: Bruce Grubbs of the Southern Baptist Sunday School Board reported that over an 18 month period that ended in 1989, more than 2,100 Southern Baptist ministers were dismissed. This was a 31 percent increase over a similar period that ended in 1985. Pastors are being released by frustrated congregations who are not pleased, and who need something or someone to blame.

Finally, consider Pastor Paul. After 30 years in the ministry, Paul is tired. Pastoring has been fulfilling, but he is now 50 years old, and dreams of retiring and doing something else. He thinks he has chronic fatigue syndrome because he feels deeply tired all the time. When he goes home, he just falls on the couch and watches television. He cannot seem to recover.

Over the years, his confidence has diminished, and he just wants to keep people in the church happy. When he gets a letter, he is afraid it might be critical, and another church controversy is just more than he could stand. The old wounds he bears from past skirmishes and friendly fire are still painful. Although Paul dreams of doing something else, his church pension plan means everything to him, so he is afraid to say anything. Feeling lonely and paranoid, he just wants to get by.

Having ministered to hundreds of pastors, as well as having my own pastorate for almost twenty-five years, I am convinced the number one dart the enemy shoots at pastors is fear. It is a versatile weapon, able to paralyze a pastor in his professional, preaching and persevering life in many ways.

Some pastors fear failure, not knowing what they would do outside of pastoring. Others are anxious about what their peers or denominational leaders might say or think if they varied from the traditions of the church. Some pastors fear what might happen if they took stands against social drinking or abortion. Some pastors are hurt, addicted to secret sins, or just burned out, and they are afraid of telling anyone, lest people see them as having problems and think them incompetent to lead the church. Many pastors are afraid of people leaving their church and putting it in financial jeopardy. As strange at it may seem, sheep have been known to use this threat to control the pastor. A pastor in Ohio even told me that he was afraid to be bold because he didn't want the devil to attack his children.

Proverbs 29:25 is right: "Fear of man will prove to be a snare." Prolonged fear in a pastor will undermine his or her confidence and squelch boldness in the Holy Spirit. Fear will make a pastor sick with burnout, depression and cynicism. It will put out a pastor's fire and cause him or her to act like a congregation's puppet, instead of a bold preacher of the Gospel.

As a layperson you can pray for your pastor's professional standing, reputation, success as a shepherd and relationship to his or her flock. You can pray that God grant your pastor a bold vision, and that this vision will be blessed and accepted in the church. Your pastor's sermons will only be as good as the prayer force behind them. You can pray for your pastor to have a deep sense of peace and fulfillment, as well as the perseverance to finish the race. Help plant a prayer hedge around your pastor that will keep him or her feeling refired, and not retired.

In Your Pastor's Honor

Have you ever wondered how the Catholic Church has existed for more than a thousand years, in nearly every nation of the world, without splitting?

Perhaps I have the answer.

In every mass ever conducted, prayers are offered for the Pope and the bishop of the diocese by name. Imagine how many prayers are lifted up for the Pope in a single week! It might just be that, because the church prays for its leaders, Satan has found no foothold to divide it.

You may never know how deeply your pastor and the members of your parsonage family appreciate the prayers you offer in their behalf.

Numbers 16 tells an interesting story. Korah, Dathan and Abiram were not happy with the conditions in their community, and they went as a group to oppose Moses and Aaron, their shepherds. They questioned Moses as their appointed leader, and they asked Moses and Aaron, "Why then do you set yourselves above the LORD's assembly?" Perhaps Korah, Dathan and Abiram felt that they were equally qualified to lead the Israelites to the promised land.

When Moses heard their opposition, he proposed a "trial by fire," telling them, "In the morning, the LORD will show who belongs to him and who is holy." When the assembly gathered in the morning, God opened up the earth and swal-

lowed Korah, Dathan and Abiram and all of their
possessions and households—hymnals and all.
They were destroyed because they spoke out
against their pastor!

The Lord seemed to take it personally when
the people spoke against the leader he appointed. Why?

I believe the office of pastor is, in a sense, rep-
resentative of God in the local church. Therefore,
the way we treat our pastors reveals some of our
respect for God. When a church fails to honor
the office of pastor—no matter who the person
is—the church dishonors God. To accuse and be-
little the pastor without praying for him or her
offends God, and when God is offended, the
ground opens up to swallow the church's blessings, effectiveness and authority in the community. In other words, if we cannot honor the pastor whom we can see, how can we honor God
whom we cannot see?

I believe a prayer hedge around the pastor
honors him or her, because the highest honor
you can give someone is to pray for them. And
where honor is given, God will bestow victory and
blessing. As a layperson, taking your pastor for
granted is a sin! The reason a few opposers can
harm a pastor is because the 95 percent of the
congregation who like and support the pastor are
not mobilized to pray for him or her. When you
build a hedge of prayer around your pastor, you
honor your pastor and you honor God.

Jonathan Edwards (1703-1758), the famous
early American preacher, once said,

> If some Christians that had been com-
> plaining about their minister had said and

acted less before men and had applied
themselves with all their might to cry to
God for their ministers—had, as it were,
risen and stormed heaven with their
humble, fervent, and incessant prayers for
them—they would have been much more
in the way of success.

A pastor not prayed for is preyed on. The
more a pastor threatens the enemy, the more severe will be the attacks. But I believe God called
your pastor to be fruitful (John 15:8). Your shepherd needs to be fulfilled and happy in his or her
work. Pastors need wisdom, anointing, rest, opportunities to share Christ, rich sermons, financial freedom, good family time, a keen sense of
fulfillment, realistic time management, vision and
creativity. As a layperson, you are the key to lifting your pastor's battle-weary hands as Aaron
and Hur lifted Moses' hands, keeping your pastor protected through all areas of ministry.

Jesus set the example for us when He prayed
for his shepherds in training, the disciples, saying,

"Holy Father, protect them by the power
of your name—the name you gave me . . .
My prayer is not that you take them out
of the world but that you protect them
from the evil one" (John 17:11,15).

Jesus also instructs us,

"Ask and it will be given to you; seek and
you will find; knock and the door will be
opened to you. For everyone who asks receives; he who seeks finds; and to him

who knocks, the door will be opened.
... how much more will your Father in
Heaven give good gifts to those who ask
him!" (Matthew 7:7-8,11).

Famous evangelist and writer E. M. Bounds
(1835-1913) states,

Air is not more necessary to the lungs
than prayer is to the preacher. It is abso-
lutely necessary for the preacher to pray.
It is an absolute necessity that the
preacher be prayed for. These two propo-
sitions are wedded into a union which
ought never to know any divorce: The
preacher must pray, the preacher must be
prayed for. It will take all the praying he
can do, and all the praying he can get
done, to meet the fearful responsibilities
and gain the largest, truest success in his
great work.[8]

Chapter Three

How to Plant a Prayer Hedge to Protect and Sustain Your Pastor

What impact could a humble cobbler and his bedridden sister possibly have on the world?

The man was William Carey, a soft-spoken, deeply conscientious shoe repairman who lived in England at the turn of the century. Patrons arrived at his modest shop in horse-drawn carriages. As he hammered on new heels, cut and glued leather and replaced worn shoe laces, he frequently looked up at a map of the world that he had tacked to the wall above his workbench.

"Who is going to carry the Good News of Jesus Christ to the unsaved millions who live in all those far-off countries on my map?" he wondered. At night, he asked his crippled sister the same question. "Who is going to go?" he asked.

God spoke, and the answer came down to one person: William Carey!

The cobbler packed up his belongings, caught a steamer and followed the needle on his compass to India where he labored for 42 years. Today, Carey and his co-workers are best remembered for having translated the Bible into 26 Indian languages and the New Testament into 25 more. Carey has been credited with leading millions to accept Jesus Christ as Lord and Savior—and for inspiring countless hundreds of young men and women around the globe to become missionaries.

At least once a week, Carey wrote his frail, bedridden sister asking her to pray . . .

But there's a key part of the story most people have never heard. At least once a week, Carey wrote his frail, bedridden sister asking her to pray for divine guidance in his efforts. Hour after hour, week after week, year after year she kept her brother's concerns before the Lord. *She* was the "secret force" in his ministry!

Within every church there are persons who, if asked, will become praying saints for your pastor. They may be shut-ins, elderly individuals who are confined to nursing homes or even persons in prison. You may find that some of your most active members will be honored to become intercessors in behalf of your pastor.

Imagine what a difference prayer can make in *your* church!

You may be asking yourself at this point, "Where do I begin? I agree with what I'm reading. I know there is great power in prayer, and I want to enlist people to pray for my pastor."

How to Equip Your Church to Pray

My goal in this chapter is to give you and your pastor some practical information you need to begin to organize a prayer force.

1. GET ORGANIZED WITH A PLAN

Begin by knowing that it will take time to plant and grow a prayer hedge. It won't grow overnight. You will need to be very intentional.

Recently, a church in Saint Louis completed a capital fund campaign that ran for three years. The entire effort was well organized. The volunteer workers followed a master chart that explained exactly what each person was to do and when. The campaign went "over the top" in reaching its goal.

When it comes to organizing a prayer effort for the pastor, most churches are as disorganized as the Keystone Cops. This isn't necessary. Properly organized, building a prayer hedge can be fun—and a very rewarding experience for each person involved.

I have helped a number of churches plant "hedges" on behalf of their pastors. So, in this book I want to save you time by outlining the basic steps I have worked out over the years.

2. SHARE YOUR INTENTIONS WITH YOUR PASTOR

Let the pastor know this is a genuine move to bless and protect, and not some devious plot to expose or oust him or her. Ask for your pastor's advice and prayer concerns, and work in close concert with his or her desires.

Use the utmost confidentiality in handling the prayer needs of the pastor and his or her family. Be sensitive to the fact that there may have been, up until now, little interest in praying for your pastor. Your sudden concern may overwhelm your pastor at first. Move slowly and compassionately for the long-term gain and not a quick emotional appeal with little quality or depth.

3. WORK WITH EXISTING PRAYER MINISTRIES

One of the easiest ways to build a prayer hedge for your pastor is to ask persons who are *already* praying in a systematic way to start praying specifically for their pastor.

Interface pastoral prayer with other prayer ministries that are already in existence. For example, you can start by asking youth groups, single's groups, women's groups, or Sunday School classes to devote part of their time to praying for the pastor. If your church has a Wednesday evening prayer meeting, be sure to include them in your plans.

4. DEVISE A PLAN FOR TRAINING YOUR HEDGE

It's likely you will find many people in your church who want to pray for their pastor, but they don't know how. They need training. Dick Eastman's book, *The Hour That Changes the World*[1] is an excellent training tool for personal and corporate prayer. In his diagram shown on page 59, he divides an hour into twelve five-minute sections. This division helps a person understand the different dimensions of prayer to promote creativity and variety in personal prayer.

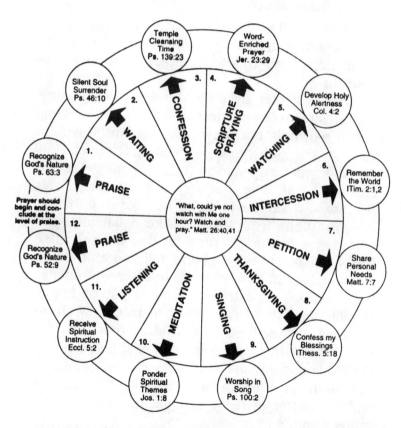

This diagram is reprinted by permission of Change The World Ministries, P.O. Box 5838, Mission Hills, CA 91345.

This twelve-step prayer plan should be applied with spiritual liberty rather than regimented legality. After using these steps for a week or two, allow your own prayer program to develop.

5. RECRUIT PEOPLE TO PRAY IN THE HEDGE

a. Start small

Start small and go for consistency and quality. As you branch out, quietly and routinely recruit people from different age-level groups in the church.

Cindy Jacobs gives helpful advice to pastors who desire to build their own hedge, based on Jesus' words in Matthew 7:7, "Ask and it will be given to you; seek and you will find; knock and the door will be opened to you." She suggests two steps: (1) *Ask*. The first step is to pray and ask the Lord to set aside personal prayer partners on your behalf. (2) *Seek*. Make a list of those whom you feel might pray for you on a regular basis. "Listen to what people tell you as they go out the door of your church or after you speak. Some will say repeatedly, 'I pray for you and your family every day.' Take time to interview these as to what they hear from God as they pray for you. If you are in the ministry, God has already set aside some who are to pray for you. Mobilizing them for effectual intercession is usually a simple matter of recognizing what God has already done."[2]

b. Look for maturity

What is James Dobson's "secret?" In the past decade, he has become one of America's most renowned pastors, reaching millions every week with his television programs, video tapes, audio cassettes, books and seminars. The demands on his time would drive most pastors to distraction, but not James!

Behind the scenes, back in Boone, North Carolina, is his 71-year-old friend and faithful intercessor, Nobel Hathaway. Each day this highly dedicated Christian layman prays for Dr. Dobson and each member of his family.

Listen to his unwavering pledge of support: "I have committed my remaining days to continue the ministry that Dr. Dobson's parents started," Hathaway explains. "Every morning before breakfast, I have a 'one-man prayer meeting' for Jim, Shirley, Danae and Ryan. I bombard the skies with prayers for the Dobsons."[3]

Amen!

Start your prayer hedge by choosing some of the most mature members of your church who are already praying. These proven and committed prayer warriors can be extremely faithful and powerful intercessors.

c. Recruit a wide range of partners

A few years ago, Mark Rutland was conducting a seminar for pastors that caused him to be on his feet during most of the meeting. The pain had become so great from a nagging bone problem in his right foot that he was unable to stand and continue. So Mark asked those pastors with the gift of healing to come forward and pray for him. Nevertheless, the pain continued.

Suddenly, a young boy with Down Syndrome walked forward from the back of the church. As he approached Dr. Rutland, he pulled out a toy gun, pointed it at the afflicted foot and said, "Bang, bang, Mark. Be healed in Jesus' name."

Immediately the pain disappeared.

That night, there was not a dry eye in the place. It just proves that sometimes the least obvious person will prove to be one of the greatest prayer warriors.

I had a similar experience while conducting a prayer seminar in Oklahoma City. The flu had gotten me down and, despite prayers being offered in my behalf, my condition was steadily growing worse. My fever escalated, and I began to feel faint.

After I preached, I came down to the altar to visit with fellow worshipers. A woman who was confined to a wheelchair rolled toward me and I reached forward to clasp her hand. Because of a speech impediment, she could barely talk. I strained to listen. This dear soul was praying for me. *Instantly,* I was healed!

In God's eyes, *every* person is capable of intercessory prayer.

I love stories like these because they illustrate in such a powerful way the sovereignty of God and his total disregard for earthly achievements or stature. He often uses "the least of these" to accomplish mighty deeds in his name. You may be surprised where you can find very dedicated intercessors.

6. ANTICIPATE SOME APATHY

A laywoman in Michigan made the appeal for prayer in her church of 200, and only two people responded. It is not easy to plant a hedge because there is apathy in the soil. Where there is no root, the prayer hedge simply cannot grow. However, don't take resistance as the final answer. Rely on the Holy Spirit and go forward with your efforts in the name of Jesus.

7. SHARE YOUR PASTOR'S VISION WITH YOUR PARTNERS

As you recruit people, share the pastor's vision with them, and give them a guide to direct their praying. Explain the goal of this prayer emphasis and tell them how important it is. You may want to distribute the *Preyed On Or Prayed For* manual which contains a prayer card for hedging in the pastor as well as step-by-step instructions on how to use it effectively. In essence, systematically develop a prayer network that will assure a long-lasting hedge.

8. NAME YOUR GROUP

You will probably want to name your special group. The men who pray for me are called the Gibborium, the Hebrew word meaning "mighty men." They were King David's elite soldiers who went with him to guard him. In one church they are called "The Watchmen." Dr. Mark Rutland has a group of intercessors called the "Elijah Force." Naming a prayer hedge gives the members a sense of mission and camaraderie.

9. SET SPECIFIC TIMES TO PRAY

Give people you recruit a time frame in which to pray. Most of us today live by schedules, and we need to schedule prayer into our lives. For example, ask someone to pray for the pastor for six weeks, or maybe for three months. Pastor Mike Bickle says that one of the main reasons people don't pray is because they do not schedule it. He's right. You will want to help your hedge members schedule their focus of prayer weekly or even daily. Encourage them to come to the church early on Sundays to lift up the pastor's hands, since Sundays are especially stressful in most pastors' lives.

Scheduling prayer is what I call "term praying." This means that you announce when the term of praying begins and ends. Doing so will help your partners have a sense of fulfillment and closure to their commitment.

A pastor in Denver simply asks two or three different laypersons each Sunday to pray with him in his study. It's his unique way of introducing them to the idea of becoming part of regular prayer efforts in his behalf.

The pastor of a large church in Washington, D.C. has enlisted 27 men to pray for him. He assigns each man to pray a particular day of the week. Then, on Monday, he has breakfast with the seven for that week—and he tells them what is before him so they can pray effectively. In addition, an adult Sunday school class prays for the pastor as part of their Sunday discipline.

You might also enlist prayer for the pastor during the service. If a layperson reads the Bible text for the sermon, have him or her say a prayer for the pastor at the close of the reading. Such modeling before the church sets a good example of praying for the pastor that the members can see and follow. If the pastor leaves town to preach a revival or attend a conference, make sure to provide special prayer prior to his or her departure and throughout the trip.

10. STAY IN TUNE TO PRAY AT ANY TIME

When was the last time you had a "close call?"

One afternoon, as I was driving my little Volkswagen home from seminary, I accidentally turned the wrong way down a one-way street. All I was thinking about was getting home. Maybe that's why I was oblivious to the traffic signals that were only visible in my rear view mirror. I had the road all to myself.

A split second later, I saw a huge truck pulling out straight into the side of my tiny Volkswagen. The other fellow hit his brakes and screeched to a halt as I frantically swerved to avoid being squashed like a bug. I experienced the true meaning of "divine intervention."

The next morning, one of my intercessors called to say that she had received a burden to ask Jesus to protect me the previous day. The woman asked, "What was going on yesterday at four o'clock?"

After I told her about my close call, we both realized that it was because of her prayers and the grace of God that I was not wiped out.

My incident in Dallas was a quarter of a century ago, but it remains a vivid memory. I am reminded of it every time I get going the "wrong way" in life and am "spared" through the prayers of one of my members.

Does your pastor need your prayers *right now?* Remember, not all prayers can be scheduled. Train your partners to be sensitive to the presence of the Holy Spirit in their lives so they can immediately pray for your pastor's special needs.

11. GIVE FEEDBACK TO YOUR PARTNERS

When possible, give your hedge feedback about answered prayers, and get feedback from them concerning what they are hearing as they pray. This will help you water and trim the hedge better. Regularly express your appreciation to persons who pray for your pastor. Doing so will make them feel genuinely good about what they are doing and will give them an incentive to continue praying. The apostle Paul was thankful he had been prayed for. He writes,

> He has delivered us from such a deadly peril, and he will deliver us. On him we have set our hope that he will continue to deliver us, as you help us by your prayers. Then many will give thanks on your behalf for the gracious favor granted us in answer to the prayers of many (2 Corinthians 1:10-11).

Suggest to your pastor that he thank your partners from the pulpit, and in the church bulletins and newsletters. In addition, he might call or write them. Such personal attention will go a long way toward retaining your most active members, reactivating partners who have become inactive and recruiting new partners.

12. IDENTIFY ALL OF THE PLACES WHERE A PRAYER HEDGE MIGHT GROW

Think creatively about various models and modes in which you can enlist people to pray. The Central Baptist Church in Bryan, Texas has deacons who take turns praying in the prayer room as their shepherd preaches.

In John Maxwell's church, Skyline Wesleyan Church in San Diego, California, the men meet with him early on Sunday morning to pray for the text, the sermon and the services. Dr. Mark Rutland meets with his hedge at 8:00 a.m. on Sundays to pray. They gather around him and pray for his protection and anointing. According to Mark, "This works!"

As a layperson, you need to plant prayer hedges all over the church in order to keep your pastor blessed and protected. Find Aarons and Hurs who will get on one side and the other and hold up your pastor's hands. Recruit them to pray. Train them so that they have content and aim, put them in position, encourage them with good feedback and results from prayer and thank them for their time.

You might designate one Sunday a year as "Pastor Appreciation Sunday," and raise "prayer pledges" for your pastor. Almost all churches have pledge campaigns to raise money for their budgets. It's every bit as important to encourage prayer for the shepherd. As the pastor is prayed for, other leaders will be honored and prayed for in the church. When your leader is honored, an atmosphere of affirmation and support will be fostered throughout your church.

13. OPEN A PRAYER ROOM IN YOUR CHURCH TO PRAY FOR YOUR PASTOR

If you already have a prayer room, you can create a special place in it to remind people to pray specifically for their pastor.

Church on the Rock in Rockwall, Texas has a prayer station in their prayer room with pictures of the pastor and church staff. It is a good idea to include a prayer guide to direct the praying in a biblical, positive way. When Larry Lea pastored Church on the Rock, he made prayer a top priority. He not only put pictures in the prayer room, he gave the following specific instructions to his intercessors. He entitled it, "How to Pray for Your Pastor."

a. Pray that the pastor's private life will be as strong as his public life.

b. Pray that nothing will violate the anointing from without or from within.

c. Pray the Lord will send in a great harvest of souls from the north, south, east and west.

d. Pray that the pastor will be delivered from unreasonably negative people.

e. Pray that the Lord will bless the church financially so the pastor can focus on ministry.

f. Pray that the Lord will place a hedge of protection around the pastor's family.

The prayer room movement is one of the fastest growing prayer expressions in the world today. More than 1,000 Southern Baptist churches have set aside a room only for prayer on an ongoing basis. Modeled after the Upper Room where the early church prayed continuously, the prayer room usually has as outside entrance and no access to the general church building. It should be comfortable and conducive to prayer. The advantages are multiple. People can sign up and come on a scheduled basis. Pertinent information can be laid out by the pastor for prayer. And the room provides a place for prayer on special occasions.

In our church, people pray in the room while I am preaching. Recently, Union Chapel Ministries in Muncie, Indiana put in a perpetual prayer room. I asked one of the staff members to tell me about the difference it had made. He said,

> *Paul said, "Pray continuously." A prayer room in the local church makes this possible.*

"Direction—we now have direction and it is wonderful!" What a marvelous way to soak a church and its leadership in prayer.

We have a vision of raising up and networking 1,000 prayer rooms by the year 2000. We hope to tie these rooms together to pray for Christian leaders and their families when in trouble, and also to pray for church planting teams in unreached nations. Just think, 1,000 prayer rooms praying 24 hours a day. That is more than 24,000 prayer hours a day! What a fantastic source of power for the pastors of our nation.

If you are interested, Bristol House has published the workbook, *Making Room to Pray*. Within its pages you will find all of the information needed to build a prayer room to intercede for your pastor and other needs in the church.

Paul said, "Pray continuously." A prayer room in the local church makes this possible.

14. HELP PROTECT YOUR PASTOR'S TIME

One of the goals of the prayer hedge is to insure that your pastor is a man or woman of God. To be a man or woman of God requires that the pastor be with God as often as possible to build his or her own prayer life.

A pastor too busy to pray is in danger of missing God's voice, but with the permission and support of the ruling board, a pastor will be much more likely to spend time before the Father in prayer.

A pastor too busy to pray is in danger of missing God's voice . . .

You may want to encourage your board to give your pastor seasons or times to go away to a place of privacy and pray. Such retreats will renew and bless your pastor in a multitude of ways. Dr. Morris Sheets at Hillcrest Church in Dallas, Texas takes two or three days a week to be alone with God.

You can also encourage your pastor to join a pastors' prayer group. More and more of these groups are springing up across the country. Pastors are meeting to pray for their cities. Such times of prayer are providing much needed support for the individual pastors as well. For example, in Austin, Texas a group of 30 pastors meets and prays from the top of a local hotel for their city. Visually, they are claiming their city for Jesus Christ.

As in your other efforts, expect some hesitation. Today is open season on pastors, and any attempt to guard or reappropriate their time will naturally be discouraged by the enemy. You may catch the vision, yet others will not see it in the same way. Remember that it takes time to burrow through a brick wall. Be persistent and keep your goals clearly in mind.

15. PRAY FOR OTHER PASTORS

Churches also need to pray for each other's pastors. After our early service at College Station, a couple in our congregation travels from church to church and prays for each pastor. As they listen, they lift the pastor up to the Lord.

Calvary Assembly in Orlando, Florida chooses one church in the Orlando area every Sunday and prays for the church and pastor. The Lord is honored when we honor the shepherds of the city. "How good and pleasant it is when brothers live together in unity! . . . For there the Lord bestows his blessing, even life forevermore" (Psalm 133:1, 3).

Seek out ways to motivate the members of your church not only to pray for your own shepherd, but also for the shepherds of other flocks.

16. ACT NOW!

Don't get bogged down early-on in developing elaborate plans. After you have touched base with your pastor to outline what you want to do, ask two or three members of your church to become founding members of your prayer group. Right away, ask them to start praying daily for your pastor and the success of your prayer group. Ask your pastor to announce what you are doing from the pulpit and invite persons who are interested to contact you. In addition, get a story about starting the group printed in your church newsletter and the Sunday worship bulletin.

Not long ago, I visited a former pastor in a Houston hospital. He confessed that he was hooked on cocaine. At one time, he was one of the best Bible teachers I knew, but he had lost everything. I asked him what happened, and he said, "I lost my prayer covering, and I was unable to stand alone." How tragic. With a well-planted prayer hedge, the story would probably have had a totally different outcome.

Remember, we are at war. The enemy comes to steal, kill, and destroy.

> For our struggle is not against flesh and blood, but against the rulers, against the authorities, against the powers of this dark world and against the spiritual forces of evil in the heavenly realms" (Ephesians 6:12).

The devil prowls around like a roaring lion looking for a pastor to devour, and his darts are literal. He fires at the flammable areas of our lives. He shoots criticism, immoral thoughts, fears of failure, unwholesome comparisons and self-doubts. He shot at the apostles in the book of Acts, and still his strategy is to shoot the leader. He tries to use power and prestige to bend a pastor toward the world. He often sets traps in counseling sessions to ensnare pastors in unhealthy relationships. He shoots barrages of flaming arrows at the pastor's spouse and children in an effort to destroy the parsonage family. He inflicts and infects with depression and attitudes of self-pity.

Satan's goal is for the pastor to be lonely, cut off and cast in a sea of despondence. Why? Revelation 12:12 answers: "He is filled with fury, because he knows that his time is short." Zechariah 13:7 tells us: "Strike the shepherd, and the sheep will be scattered." If the pastor is listless and visionless, the sheep will be as well. Therefore, the enemy's assault is on the shepherd. No pastor is exempt. Pastors of large churches or small churches, holy men and holy women are all vulnerable to his attacks. Honest pastors are tempted to become otherwise.

The pressure never ceases, and it won't until we enter the kingdom of heaven. We are in enemy territory, and we need coverings of prayer to stand and even stand some more. The more effective a pastor is, the more he or she will be attacked.

A Word of Caution to Pastors

C. Peter Wagner has an excellent chapter in his book *Prayer Shield* on receiving intercession. As pastors, we must become more open to ask for prayer and also to receive it. The noted author lists several reasons why we often won't seek out prayer ourselves.[4] The following is a summary of these roadblocks to accepting prayer.

A. IGNORANCE

Often, as pastors we just don't think to ask for prayer on a regular basis. We may ask for prayer on special occasions, for specific preaching missions or at troubled times in our ministry, but it may not be something we think about needing on a regular basis. We will ask for financial support or for time commitments from our flock before we will ask them to pray for us daily or weekly. It may not have been emphasized in seminary, or it's not the traditional thing to do. It is amazing to me how much has been written on recovery and personal development for pastors, yet the idea of prayer for us has been sorely neglected.

The book by George Barna that I have referred to several times contains excellent information about senior pastors across the country and where we stand as a profession in our own eyes as well as in the eyes of our congregations. He found some startling statistics about frustrations, fears and struggles many of us face in our ministries. He even offered some reasons for such conditions as well as some possible solutions. But nowhere in his analysis did prayer for pastors show up.

It seems that raising up prayer hedges for the shepherds of our nation is a solution yet to be discovered or taken seriously. I believe that laypersons will start praying for us when we take the initiative to make them aware that we cannot survive without their covering.

B. RUGGED INDIVIDUALISM

Many of us are not prayed for because we like to think of ourselves as being rugged individualists. We feel we are supposed to have the answers. "Look to us, and we will pray and speak the message from God." Fallen leaders abound who tried to be self-sufficient and were not open to expose needs for prayer. Jimmy Swaggart reflected on this when he said,

I think this is the reason that I did not find the victory I sought because I did not seek the help of my brothers and my sisters in the Lord. . . . If I had sought the help of those that love me, with their added strength, I look back now and know that the victory would have been mine.[5]

We must repent of being isolated into thinking we can do it on our own. If we are to receive prayer, we need to be willing to step beyond the chancel rail to say, "Pray for me." We must be willing to share our heart with a core of people we trust. There are some we can share general requests with and some we can share more intimately with. But the bottom line is, if we are not willing to communicate our personal and ministerial needs, we cannot receive prayer. Barna's assessment is painfully true when he states,

In the typical church, it is impossible for the pastor to be truly transparent about the struggles he endures with people within the church, within his family or within the ministry overall. Consequently, most pastors tell us they feel lonely in ministry. While they have many friends and acquaintances with whom they can share a good laugh and a pleasant evening, they have few people with whom they can share their hearts.[6]

At College Station, I have several levels of intercessors. A small group of men prays with me intimately. Some 20 men pray for me during Sunday's ministry. I meet with them on Sunday

mornings and share my text and my goals so
they can pray effectively. In our prayer room,
there is a recorder on which I share my needs
and concerns on a weekly basis, and I have an
Aaron and Hur Society that prays for me. On
special occasions, my close friends in the ministry pray for me. But it is up to me to communicate with all my intercessors, or they don't
know how to pray.

C. FEAR

For many of us, fear is an obstacle to receiving prayer. We are afraid that what we say can
be used against us. We're also afraid that if we
let our people see our weaknesses and needs—
our humanness—they will lose confidence in us.
And what if our prayer requests are misunder-
stood or taken the wrong way? Fear to ask for
help when needed has caused too many pastors
I know to end up living lives of regret.

Every time I drive north out of Dallas on a
certain highway, I can't help but recall a beautiful red brick church where a terrible tragedy
occurred. I feel sick when I see the steeple of that
once dynamic church, because I know that intercessory prayer could have rewritten history for
the pastor, John, and his wife, Betty.

Maybe it was because Betty was raised in
upstate New York and didn't know how to relate
to Texans. All I know is that she never felt accepted, and was constantly battling depression.

Their story had all of the ingredients of a real-
life tragedy.

Her condition had gotten so bad that, just before Christmas, John had to hospitalize Betty for

an overdose of sleeping pills. After returning home, she sensed that everyone in the church knew what had happened. One Sunday, she overheard a layman telling his son that she was "nuts."

The next morning, she confronted John with her feelings. "Honey, the people in the hospital were so nice to me. I wonder why the people in our church treat me so badly." John reached out and embraced Betty. She placed her head on his shoulder and began to cry. A few minutes later, as John backed out of the driveway to attend a two-day pastors' confer-

> *"I wonder why the people in our church treat me so badly."*

ence in Dallas, Betty decided to write him a letter that would explain why and how she wanted to end her loneliness.

"URGENT: CALL YOUR CHURCH." That's all that was written on the note that was passed to John the following morning as he ate breakfast with fellow pastors. When he returned the call, his secretary told him the grim news. Late the previous evening, Betty had entered the sanctuary and taken what the letter found by her body described as her "last communion," a massive dose of sleeping pills.

Today, John is 61. He lives alone, praying that his church will let him stay until he retires. He deeply regrets being reluctant to ask for prayer for his wife when so many others in his congregation had what then seemed like more pressing needs.

Imagine what might have happened if John had not been afraid to ask his members to embrace their pastor and his wife with prayer!

The tragic thing about this situation is that despite the fact his church would surely have been willing to support their pastor and his wife through their crisis, he was unable to ask for or accept help because he feared exposure and embarrassment. Think of the suffering and loss that might have been avoided, or at least lessened, if John had been able to share his burden with a group of dedicated intercessors and receive prayer. At least he would now be able to know that he had done everything possible to have saved Betty.

As pastors, we must not let fear have its way. Prayer for the pastor is not only proven helpful, it is biblical. We should be afraid of what might happen if we don't get prayed for! Ask God to give you prayer partners you can trust without fear.

D. SPIRITUAL ARROGANCE

Pride can be so subtle in a pastor, especially the longer we serve and the more "experienced" we are. No pastor is immune to it, yet we must repent of spiritual arrogance.

Not long ago I was struggling with an issue of not trusting God in terms of church leadership. As a recovering co-dependent, I feel a need to be in control, and I was worried and anxious that I might lose that control in a certain matter. One day the most unstable member of our church came to my office to "encourage" me. Usually, I don't take appointments with her, but that day she managed to slip in. In the middle of her visit she said, "You need to trust God." Ouch! She was right. Although she didn't know it, she had been sent by God to remind me that he is the one in control. I got the message and I repented.

Asking people to pray for us requires vulnerability and openness. It is the very dynamic that can protect us from arrogance, pride and self-sufficiency.

One of my favorite ways to receive prayer is to ask godly older saints to pray for me. To kneel in front of a 70- or 80-year-old saint and receive prayer is a most blessed experience. Whenever I meet such a person, I ask them to kneel with me right then and there. Being a pastor is such a challenging task, it requires all the help we can get.

E. UNDUE HUMILITY

Finally, Wagner says that undue humility can prevent us from being prayed for. He states,

> The logic goes something like this: 'I am no better than anyone else in the body of Christ. We are all sinners saved by grace. God loves all of his children equally. He does not love me any more than the others. Why, then, should I expect to receive this powerful intercession when so many of my church members do not have the same privilege? Instead of building a special team of prayer partners for myself, might it not be better to just encourage all church members to pray for each other?"[7]

Where does a "terminally ill" pastor with *undue humility* turn for help?

The pastor of a church in Baltimore wasn't the kind of person who found it easy to share personal problems with his congregation. However, when writing to a former member who had moved to Seattle some 21 years earlier, he felt safe enough to confide in her the seriousness of his physical illness. He trusted the woman to keep his secret—and he was right.

What the pastor had no way of knowing was that the once loyal member of his church would make it her mission in life to sustain him through her prayers. Not only did she pray for him every morning and evening, she sent a letter to his post office box *each day* for two and one-half years marked "personal."

She stopped sending the letters only after he wrote to let her know his disease had gone into remission—and that he had experienced a complete recovery!

What was in her daily letters? A "Get Well" card, a verse of scripture and a handwritten copy of the prayerful petition that she had raised to God that day for her former pastor's speedy recovery.

"She was my intercessor," he said, "my link to a Healing Power that was greater than any of us can ever imagine. Even though I never thought of asking her to pray for me, I am alive today because one person believed with all her heart that Jesus Christ could make me whole again."

George Barna is right in asking,

> Is it time to evaluate how satisfactorily the current church ministry system cares for pastors? Do we need to determine how

well we are looking after the financial, emotional, and spiritual welfare of our spiritual leaders . . . ?[8]

As pastors, we must repent of not alarming people to pray for us in our special calling. True, we are like everyone else, but we have a call to preach and lead the church. For this we need much prayer. Furthermore, when people pray for us, they get to go with us when we go to prisons or hospitals. Our intercessors should become a part of our day-to-day ministry and preaching. When this happens, we will truly become joint-heirs in the service of Jesus Christ. When they pray for us, they reap the same blessing that we do when souls are saved and lives are changed. Our victory becomes their victory because they made it possible. We serve together in the harvest.

Practice saying, "Please pray for me. Here's how!"

How to Care for Your Hedge

Someone in your church may take this book and plant a prayer hedge around you. They may actually recruit, train and encourage people to lift up your hands for protection and blessing. If so, these prayer warriors will stand in the gap for your preaching. They will call out to God on behalf of your spouse and children. Some will even fast and stay up late praying for you. If such a hedge is raised up around you, let me encourage you to water and nurture it so that all will flourish.

Here are some ways to maintain your prayer hedge:

1. ENCOURAGE THE PRAYER HEDGE FROM THE PULPIT.

Let everyone know that you need a prayer hedge, and that you fully support its formation.

2. MEET WITH THE "SPARK PLUGS" WHO WILL BUILD YOUR HEDGE.

Share your ideas and build a close rapport with those in charge of creating it. Affirm them in what they are doing.

3. GIVE THEM INFORMATION WITH WHICH TO PRAY, SUCH AS LARRY LEA'S INSTRUCTIONS.

Be specific about your needs. Include your visions, goals, preaching texts, study times and stressful times of counseling or ministry. Share with them to the degree of trust that you assign to the various levels in your own intercessory circles. Look for ways to encourage them to pray God's Word over you. You may even want to write a prayer guide specifically for them.

4. GIVE THEM FEEDBACK CONCERNING THE RESULTS OF THEIR PRAYERS.

My hedge prays for me when I go out on special prayer missions. I give them my schedule and tell them the actual time I am going to speak. I know that when I stand up, they go to their knees.

When I get back, I share with them what happened and they become a part of my ministry.

They are excited to pray for me and then hear how God responded!

5. PRAY FOR THEM.

C. Peter Wagner keeps pictures of his intercessors in his Bible, and he prays over their faces. I often take photos of my intercessors to the altar with me so I can pray for them.

6. DON'T EXPECT TO REPAY THEM.

It would be almost impossible to measure the worth of their prayers, and their reward will be great in heaven. But do find ways of thanking them. My wife and I have our intercessors over for burnt offerings (hamburgers and hot dogs) once or twice a year. They love it, and I love serving them. I continually tell my hedge what they mean to me.

Care for your hedge tenderly, whether it is big or small, if you are blessed to have one. Their prayers will have great results.

John Maxwell, pastor of Skyline Wesleyan Church in San Diego, has developed an excellent resource video and audiocassette tape called *The Pastor's Prayer Partners.* He has recruited more than 100 Aarons and Hurs who pray for him, and he knows how important it is to keep his hedge. John meets with them four times a year, three times for breakfast and one time for an all-day prayer partners' retreat where they eat together, play together, learn together and above all pray together. He meets with one fourth of them on Sunday morning before the service and he has lunch once a month with his leading intercessor. This dynamic pastor cares very well for his hedge and his hedge stands tall and strong around him. He knows in his heart that he is a prayed-for pastor.

To request a copy of the video and audiocassette tapes, call the church secretary at Skyline Wesleyan Church: (619) 460-5000.

What Should You Pray?

They seemed like the perfect couple . . .

Ken was captain of his college football team. Linda was his favorite cheerleader. They were married a few weeks before Ken entered seminary. Ken's professors called him "brilliant."

In 1985, Ken became pastor of a fledgling church in one of the wealthiest coastal cities of southern California. Within a year, the membership had doubled and ground was being broken for a new sanctuary. During the same time, Linda became the director of marketing of a small computer company. With her help, sales quadrupled.

Things kept moving upward until Ken hit 40. The middle-aged pastor needed affirmation that he was still as handsome, still as "in demand" as he was in his 20s. Linda, five years Ken's junior, was just hitting her peak in the professional world. Except for regularly attending Sunday School and church, she had "a life of her own."

Circumstances could not have been better for Samantha, a 29-year-old bit part player in the movies who was anxious to establish her independence from her husband, a wealthy screenwriter who had developed "other interests." When Samantha started coming to Ken for counseling, she turned on the charm. So did he. Soon they were playing tennis and having lunch together and on and on.

As one member of the church observed, they "bonded."

When Ken began paying less attention to Linda, she devoted more time to traveling with the just-divorced president of her company. They became what the church secretary described as "inseparable."

> *Pastors with problems need prayer, not gossip.*

As a courtesy to the once happily married couple, their church offered to pay for counseling. "The only counseling I need is from a divorce attorney," Ken said. Linda, realizing the relationship was severely damaged, agreed. "We've become the gossip of the entire community," she said. "It's best to end it now, before the church has to suffer any more embarrassment."

Most members saw the pastor and his wife starting to drift apart, but no one did anything to try and keep them together. Speaking on behalf of the church, one of the lay leaders said, "We simply didn't know what to do!"

Pastors with problems need *prayer*, not gossip. The shepherd of your flock must not be taken for granted, lest he be deceived by the enemy. The members of Ken's church would have preferred to use prayer to combat the forces of evil that divided their pastor and his wife.

They didn't know how. They didn't know *what* to pray! In such circumstances, it's imperative

that laypersons pray during their pastor's temptation—before there is a serious problem.

Prayer is not just a "rip cord" for emergen-
cies. It is the means for grace for a Christian.

You and your fellow members need to know
how to pray BEFORE there is an attack. You
don't wait until the enemy is coming over the hill
before you teach soldiers how to load and shoot
their guns. Such training is given at boot camp—
well ahead of the battle!

So, *how* should you pray?

The following are a number of sample prayers
that are based on Ephesians 6. Each one was
written with a specific need in mind. You can use
them one at a time, or pray all of them in the
order you feel is best for the spiritual needs of
your pastor.

Sample Prayers Based on Ephesians 6 and Other Scriptures

1. I thank you Father that your eyes are on
my shepherd and your ears are attentive to my
pastor's prayers and your face is against those
who plot evil against my pastor (1 Peter 3:12).
For I know that in all things you work for the
good of _____ who loves you (Romans 8:28).

Will you not graciously give my pastor this
city for Christ? And who can accuse this pastor
who is daily interceded for by Christ Jesus? (Romans 8:32-34). Therefore, in all things my pastor is more than a conqueror (Romans 8:37).
Thank you, God.

2. Lord, we pray for discernment in exposing
any schemes of the enemy against our pastor.
Show us how to pray against all powers of this

dark world and the spiritual forces of darkness in heavenly realms. And, Lord, protect us as we wage warfare on behalf of our pastor (Ephesians 6:11-12). Amen.

3. Father, I thank you that no weapons formed against my pastor will prosper. Every tongue raised against my shepherd will be cast down. Rumors and gossip will be turned aside. For _____ will be still before the Lord and wait on you. My pastor will dwell in the shadow of the Most High God and will be delivered from terror, darts of doubt, and diseases (Psalm 91:5-6). Set your angels about my pastor (Psalm 91:11) and no power of the enemy shall harm _____ (Luke 10:19). Thank God forevermore!

4. Lord, let _____ have a discerning mind to prioritize the precious minutes in the day. Let my pastor discern what is most important and be guarded against the tyranny of the urgent (2 Corinthians 11:14; 1 John 4:1).

5. Father, allow my pastor to glory only in the cross (Galatians 6:14). Keep my pastor from pride and pity. Let the cross be our reason for ministry. Amen.

6. Renew my pastor in the Holy Spirit. Let my pastor wait and mount up with wings (Isaiah 40:27-31). Quicken my shepherd's body with the Holy Spirit (Romans 8:11). Renew _____'s vision and confidence (1 John 5:13-14). Revive my pastor's boldness to stand in strong personal conviction (Acts 4:32). Amen.

7. Jesus, keep my pastor holy in every way (1 Peter 1:16). Protect my shepherd from seducing spirits especially when he or she is tired and hard-pressed. Give _____ comrades to help protect my pastor, and to share with in personal holiness (James 4:7). As my pastor draws near to you, draw near to my pastor (James 4:8). Cancel the power of sin to have no effect (Ephesians 1:22). Amen.

8. I pray that the eyes of my pastor may be enlightened to know the hope to which we are called and know the riches of our glorious inheritance in the saints. Let my pastor know the incomparable great power which is in us who believe (Ephesians 1:18-19). Let _____ see the full revelation of Jesus Christ (Galatians 1:12) and place in this pastor a desire to know Christ and the power of his resurrection (Philippians 3:10). Amen.

9. Lord, deliver Pastor _____ from the tyranny of the unfinished. Grant my pastor a sense of fulfillment and the personal joy of Jesus (1 Timothy 6:6; John 15:11). Amen.

10. Lord, as our shepherd spends quiet time with you, shed your love abroad in his or her heart. Let my pastor know how much he or she is loved (Romans 5:5). In Jesus' name let the love of God be my pastor's mainstay in ministry. So be it!

11. Lord, I lift up the hands of my pastor and his or her family. Place them in the shelter of the Most High to rest in the shadow of the Almighty. I will say of the Lord, you are their refuge and fortress. You will preserve their family time. You will cover their home. Your faithfulness will meet their financial needs in Christ Jesus (Philippians

4:19). You will command your angels to guard them as they travel and win the lost. You have said, "I will be with them in trouble, I will deliver them and honor them and with a long life, I will satisfy them and show them my salvation" (Psalm 91). In Jesus' name I cancel all assignments of the enemy against them (Matthew 6:10). Amen.

12. In Jesus' name I speak to church hurts, abuse and ungrateful forces to move. I speak to mountains of criticism and inordinate expectations to be cast into the sea. I speak to stress, excessive phone counseling and fatigue to be cast into the sea, and I believe every need, vision, and dream of _____'s will be completed (Mark 11:22-24; Philippians 4:19). Amen.

13. Forgive those who hurt _____ and speak against my pastor, and may he or she walk in forgiveness (Ephesians 4:32, 5:1). Guard my pastor from futile thinking (Ephesians 4:17) and a vain imagination. Let every thought be taken captive to obey Christ (2 Corinthians 10:3-5).

14. Lord Jesus, I know that in the course of pastoring, _____ is thrilled over conversions and changed lives, yet I also realize that my pastor hears bad news and sad stories and ministers to those who are dying. Therefore, keep my shepherd ever before your face in worship (Matthew 4:10). Let my pastor see you and enjoy your presence ever more (Psalm 112:7). Let goodness and mercy follow my pastor all the days of his or her life (Psalm 23:6) and let my pastor's cup overflow (Psalm 23:5). Amen.

15. In Jesus' name we bind the fear of failure and the fear of humankind (John 14:1). Let _____'s confidence not be eroded by the daily resistance to the gospel or his or her vision. Allow my pastor to fear God more than people. Amen.

16. Father, heal my shepherd's heart of any grief caused by ministry. Bestow on my pastor a crown of beauty instead of ashes and anoint him or her with the oil of gladness instead of mourning. Clothe my shepherd with a garment of praise instead of a spirit of depression. I call my pastor an oak of righteousness, a planting of the Lord to display your splendor (Isaiah 61:3). Amen.

17. Jesus, you said, "Do not let your hearts be troubled. Trust in God; trust also in me . . . Peace I leave with you; my peace I give you" (John 14:1, 27). Apply these promises to _____. Let my pastor know the plans you have for him or her, plans to prosper, plans to give hope and a future (Jeremiah 29:11). Amen.

18. Keep my pastor in the midst of good and exciting worship. Keep my pastor from the traditions of men and religion which hold the form of godliness, but deny its power (2 Timothy 3:5). Give _____ a vision of heaven (Isaiah 6; Revelation 4). Amen.

19. With my shield of faith I cover my shepherd's mind to quench all flaming darts of doubt or vain imagination or mental distractions (Mark 6:5-6). Let the mind of Christ be strong in my pastor. Amen.

20. Lord, I stand against the enemies of my pastor's prayer life—"busyness" (Acts 6:2-4), compulsions, compromise (Acts 5), unnecessary phone calls, chronic counselees, fatigue, sleepiness (Matthew 26:41), appetites, television, late meetings, over-commitments and doubt. Let nothing hinder _____'s time with you. Let my pastor rise up to seek you (Mark 1:35), pray with other pastors (Acts 1:14), and pray without ceasing (1 Thessalonians 5:17). Give my pastor the time, the desire and the place to pray (Acts 16:16). I rebuke in the name of Jesus any distractions from my pastor's devotional life (Mark 5:36). Amen.

21. Send the spirit of prayer upon _____ (Acts 1:8; Romans 8:26). Send others to join us in praying for our pastor (1 Timothy 2:1-8). Amen.

22. Lord, keep my pastor in the fear of God. Let my pastor not fear people (Proverbs 19:23). Give _____ boldness to confront sin and church controllers. Honor my pastor's stand for you. Come to my pastor's rescue. I claim Psalm 35 for my shepherd.

23. Lord, use _____ to renew our denomination (Proverbs 18:16). Use my pastor in an effective way to promote evangelism and holiness. Grant favor for fruitfulness. Keep my pastor from meetings for the sake of meetings. Redeem the time so as to use my pastor's abilities in the most productive manner. Amen.

24. Lord give my pastor favor with his or her peers (Proverbs 11:4). Keep my pastor from comparing him or herself with other pastors, churches or salary packages. Guard my pastor's heart from competition and unhealthy ambitions (2 Corinthians 10:18). Deliver _____ from the numbers trap, and give my pastor a genuine concern for lost souls (Luke 19:10). Lord, you advance my pastor. Let my pastor not be caught up in any political quicksand; keep only Jacob's ladder, not a career ladder, before my pastor (Genesis 28:12). Amen.

25. Jesus, dominate _____'s ministry to make people become like you and not like a denominational facsimile (Colossians 1:28). Amen.

26. Give my shepherd deep convictions and moral stands to reflect your holiness (Proverbs 4:20-27). Let my pastor not compromise truth, yet spread truth in love to address all social injustice and prejudice of any kind. Amen.

27. Let _____ trust in the Lord with all his or her heart. In all my pastor's ways may you be acknowledged and therefore, my pastor's paths made straight (James 1:5).

28. Bless my pastor with rich study time (Acts 6:4; 2 Timothy 2:15).

29. As _____ preaches, let him or her proclaim Jesus Christ (Colossians 1:28). Let my pastor's preaching be in the energy of the Holy Spirit. May we be presented to you, Father, holy and blameless as a result of my pastor's preaching. Amen.

30. Jesus, bless my pastor's preaching. Let my pastor preach Jesus Christ. Let my pastor preach a revelation of Christ (1 Peter 1:7). And give my pastor ample opportunities to proclaim you (Colossians 4:3-4).

31. As your anointing teaches _____ , teach us and admonish us in truth. Let your anointing be strong and powerful to convert the lost and convict the sinful (Luke 4:18; 1 John 2:27).

32. Lord by your Holy Spirit, anoint _____ to preach, and bring apostolic results (Acts 2:37). Let people be cut to the heart and accept Jesus Christ. Amen.

33. As my pastor speaks the Word, let signs and wonders follow confirming it (Mark 16:20). Let the sick be healed; let the oppressed be set free. Anoint _____ with the truth (Matthew 16:17). With you, Lord, all things are possible.

34. Lord, as you have promised, grant my beloved shepherd lasting fruit (Malachi 3:11; John 15:16). Let my pastor's converts become disciples who in turn disciple. Bless my pastor with disciples who grow in the grace and knowledge of Jesus Christ.

35. God, I say that _____ will stand firm. Nothing will move my pastor (1 Corinthians 15:58). May my pastor always give him or herself fully to your work because my pastor's labor is not in vain.

36. O Lord, take my pastor's hand so that he or she will not fear. Lead my pastor through difficult times. Let my pastor know that you are near and that you are my pastor's God. My pastor will not be dismayed. You will strengthen my pastor and help and uphold him or her with your righteous right hand (Isaiah 41:10).

37. O God, allow _____ to enter your rest (Hebrews 4; Matthew 11:28). Put your yoke on my pastor. When my pastor is heavily laden or burdened, may he or she find comfort and peace in you, refreshed and renewed by your power in every aspect of my pastor's life.

38. Father I thank you for _____ and for my pastor's call and gifts (Colossians 1:3-6). I praise you for sending such a shepherd for my soul! To you belong honor and glory. You are worthy, our Lord and God, to receive glory and honor and power, for you created all things, and by your will they were created and have their being (Revelation 4:11). Amen.

39. Lord make my pastor strong and filled with courage for every task (Joshua 1). Let my pastor lead us to inherit our city for you. Thank you for being with _____ .

40. In Jesus' name, _____ shall fight the good fight of faith, fleeing from evil to God by pursuing righteousness, godliness, faith, love, endurance and gentleness (1 Timothy 6:12). I praise you, Lord, that you have taken hold of this special shepherd in the personal experience of eternal life. Amen.

Finally, EXPECT all that you have prayed, STAND behind your pastor, girding him or her in prayer, and YIELD to the Spirit for other areas of prayer and intercession!

Chapter Four

Good News for Pastors: Prayer Hedges Are in Bloom!

How close to the "edge" are some pastors running?

At a breakfast in Amarillo that concluded a pastor's conference Dr. Mark Rutland and I had been leading, a pastor came forward to express his appreciation. I sensed by the look on his face and the tone of his voice that our meeting had been a significant influence on his life.

He mustered the courage to reveal what it really meant.

"I have a gun in the car," he said. "I was planning on taking my life. Things seemed so bad I had no intention of returning home. Your prayers have given me a new perspective on my ministry. This morning, I am going back to my family and my church. I will give them everything God has to offer!"

There *is* power in prayer.

If the Holy Spirit can use just one prayer to change the life of a deeply troubled pastor in west Texas, imagine the power of mobilizing a *daily* force of intercessory prayers going up in behalf of your own pastor. I can introduce you to hundreds of ministers who are living proof that a diligent, organized, consistent prayer hedge can be a mighty force in *your* pastor's life and ministry. Just as Aaron and Hur held up Moses' hands in Exodus 17, you, as a layperson, can hold up your pastor's hands.

Every pastor wants to lead his or her church to take their city for God

How should you start? First, you can pray for your pastor's protection from "friendly fire," the perils of New Testament leadership and Satan's attacks on his or her life. Your pastor can be prayed for and not preyed on.

Second, you can pray for your pastor to be blessed in every respect. Pastors want to see lives changed by the gospel of Jesus Christ. They want to see people respond as they preach and counsel. Pastors want and need the power of the Holy Spirit to enable them to live holy lives and do signs and wonders. There is no greater joy than to pray for persons and see them be healed! Every pastor wants to lead his or her church to take their city for God, and to grow in numbers to spread justice and righteousness in the land.

A happy pastor is one who sees his or her congregation walking in the reality of who they are in Jesus Christ.

Until every minister of the gospel is blessed and protected by prayer as the New Testament pastors were, the church will remain a crippled institution to some degree. By neglecting to pray for its leaders, we are hindering what should be the most powerful force in our country today. It is possible, through prayer, for pastors today to see the same kinds of supernatural results that were common in the early church—and some pastors are!

Prayer hedges work. A dynamic, consistent group of intercessors around your pastor can make all the difference in your pastor's life and ministry.

In this chapter, I will provide you with some examples from the Bible and from contemporary churches of successful hedges in action. I pray that more and more success stories will replace the stories of despair in so many local churches. I relate these in the areas of the pastor's private life, personal life, praise life, prayer life, professional life, preaching life and persevering life.

The Pastor's Private Life

Should "soft porn" be allowed on TV? I'm talking about top rated programs like "NYPD Blue" that show completely nude couples romping in bed.

Rev. Don Wildmon got so upset with what he saw on TV that he founded the American Family Association to fight industry insiders who are dishing out a steady stream of sex, crime and violence. Wildmon hired his son, Tim, to join his efforts.

Both men have come under repeated attacks for their public stands against filth and perversion on TV. Don and Tim need prayer protection from the local church for their private lives.

Tim wrote in a newsletter to his supporters:

> One Wednesday, our pastor asked me to share my family's needs with the group he had assembled to pray and worship. So I did. That sort of thing isn't as easy for me as it is for others. I don't think my reluctance is a matter of pride so much as it is that I have been around more than my share of "woe is me" Christians. Frankly, I don't enjoy being around those folks. I don't think a "woe is me" attitude is pleasing to the Lord.
>
> So, I took a few minutes at prayer meeting and shared that my wife and I felt that our family has been under fire from the enemy, physically and spiritually.
>
> We prayed, and I left that evening with a real sense that God was telling me there are times when it is necessary for Christian soldiers who get wounded to call on other believers to surround them with intercessory prayer to help turn back the enemy.
>
> This spiritual bonding to a group of believers is one of the greatest benefits of commitment to the local church.

Thanks, Tim, for a wonderful testimony to the power of prayer!

In Acts 12, King Herod arrested Christians in an effort to persecute the church. He had already had James, the brother of John, put to death when he arrested Pastor Peter to do him harm. We read in verse 5, "So Peter was kept in prison, but the church was earnestly praying to God for him." Peter had a prayer hedge in full bloom around his private life. Every home church in the city was praying for him. What a powerful shield of protection around this pastor, the leader of the early church!

The Bible says he was sleeping between two soldiers, bound by two chains. Not exactly the Jerusalem Hilton, but Peter was at peace. In fact, when the angel came to release him, Peter was sleeping so soundly that the angel had to hit Peter on the side just to wake him up! As the angel led him out of the inner cell into the city, Peter, who had thought he was seeing a vision, said, "Now I know without a doubt that the Lord sent his angel and rescued me from Herod's clutches and from everything the Jewish people were anticipating."

Peter's private life was no doubt spared serious harm because the church prayed. Prayer hedges work to keep the pastor in perfect peace, and they keep angels on duty to deliver and assist them.

The Pastor's Personal Life

"Money talks," but will it buy *silence?*

When Ted accepted the pastorate of a church in the Houston area, he told his wife, Delores, that it was going to be a "challenge greater than any we've ever tackled." The long-established church was in serious financial trouble. It had been a large church with a huge debt load. The congregation had split five times in the past ten years. A number of key contributors had transferred to other churches, leaving a handful of "big money" people to pay the enormous stack of monthly bills. After examining the books, the new pastor saw there were three families whose gifts were critical to making ends meet.

Things were going fine until Ted discovered that one of his most powerful contributors was living in sin. The pastor arranged a private meeting with the man and confronted the layman with the eye-witness account of his transgressions with another man.

The wealthy layman refused to repent. He said, "Preacher, that's my *personal* life. You're risking embarrassing me in front of my family, and you are jeopardizing my support of the church."

The following week, a woman whose livelihood depended on the wealthy layman stood up and called for a "vote of confidence" for Ted be taken in two months. The motion passed, and Ted felt a noose tightening around his neck.

That night, the pastor and his wife went home devastated. "If this is what 'ministry' is about," Ted said, "Who needs it?!"

As the couple sat crying, car after car began to arrive at their home. Soon some 40 people crowded into their living room. They brought in food and drinks, then placed their arms around Ted and Delores and prayed for them like the early church prayed in Acts over Paul's stoned body. They sang, worshiped God and gave their pastor a *true* vote of confidence. That was 10 years ago.

"If those people hadn't come by and prayed, I might not be a pastor today," Ted says. "Their prayers made all the difference!"

As we see in the book of Acts, to be true to his or her calling, a pastor must confront sin head-on. The true nature of the gospel is to call the devious areas of people's lives into question and offer them a new life through belief in God. Accepting Jesus Christ as Lord means men and women *must* repent!

The book of Acts reveals that pastors confront as well as comfort. The nature

> *Pastors proclaim the gospel of Jesus Christ and call men and women to repentance, but some people do not want to repent.*

of the gospel is to confront sin and systems of religion and tradition which hinder the purpose of God. As in Acts, pastors proclaim the gospel of Jesus Christ and call men and women to repentance, but some people do not want to repent. They resist the pastor's plea.

The Pastor's Praise Life

"Terry, where do you get all your energy?"

A lot of pastors and laypersons ask me that question. They want to know how I keep such a tight schedule and "get my cup filled" as I'm racing from one priority to the next.

It's as simple as 1, 2, 3.

First, my intercessors are constantly praying for me. Throughout the day, I visualize each person who has let me know that he or she will be lifting me up to the Lord. The power that is released to me through their prayers serves as my "spiritual dynamo."

Second, I listen to "praise tapes." I keep a cassette player and a stack of audiocassettes on the nightstand by my bed. When I awaken, I hit the "play" button. Thus, I begin each day in worship. When I jog, I wear a headset and listen to inspirational messages and Christian music. When I am in the car, I let its privacy serve as my very own sanctuary.

Third, I read about the *good* things in life. I read daily devotionals that are testimonials of persons whose lives have been transformed through belief in Jesus Christ. Their stories personalize the presence of the Holy Spirit in our lives. Any time I start to get a bit "down," I can quickly recall the account of a person who had it a lot rougher than me and found a way to overcome his or her adversities.

My hedge prays that I will keep worship as a priority in my life. I do my part by listening to and reading materials that keep praise of God ever before me.Praise makes a BIG difference in my life, and it can in yours!

When it comes to worship, pastors need a prayer support. David, a great shepherd, was also one of the greatest worship leaders in the Bible. Yet, as a leader, he was severely attacked often. Many times in Psalms, he cries out to God about his enemies. He writes,

O Lord, how many are my foes!
How many rise up against me! . . .
My thoughts trouble me and I am
distraught
at the voice of the enemy,
at the stares of the wicked;
for they bring down suffering upon
me. . . .
Fear and trembling have beset me;
horror has overwhelmed me
(Psalms 3:1; 55:2-5).

David was pursued by Saul and others even from within his own family. Yet David is noted for his strong worship in the Psalms. He exclaims,

I will extol the Lord at all times;
his praise will always be on my lips.
My soul will boast in the LORD;
let the afflicted hear and rejoice. . . .
I will praise you as long as I live,
and in your name I will lift up my
hands (Psalms 34:1-2; 63:4).

In the face of leadership perils, David's emotional cup overflowed! Why?

I believe it is because David had a supportive hedge called the "gibborium," the Hebrew word meaning "mighty men." In 1 Chronicles 11-16, some of these "mighty men" are listed. There were about 600 of them, and they stayed with David during his entire rule as king. They went where he went, stayed where he stayed, fought for him and even tried to refresh him with a drink from the pool of Bethlehem. With the help of these mighty men, he took Jebus, later to become Jerusalem, or the city of David. David was kept safe by these men, and they were a source of blessing.

One of the most touching scenes in all the Scriptures is when David is getting ready to die. He says farewell in 1 Chronicles 24, and his "mighty men," old and scarred from battles, are there by his side. Shepherd David had a protective hedge that enabled him to stay strong in his personal and corporate worship of God, even under attack from his enemies. Prayer hedges keep pastors refreshed by the presence of God. Amasai, one of David's mighty men, said,

> "We are yours, O David!
>   We are with you, O Son of Jesse!
> Success, success to you,
>   and success to those who help you,
>   for your God will help you"
> (1 Chronicles 12:18).

Is someone saying this to your pastor?

Personally, I find that as my people pray for me, I worship God often. In the early mornings, I always get up and begin the day by giving thanks for his many mercies.

The Pastor's Prayer Life

"My life was miserable!"

Building one of the largest congregations in the world was taking its toll on Dr. Paul Cho, pastor of the Full Gospel Central Church in Seoul, Korea.

What was the problem? His severe health crisis was due to exhaustion from overwork. He fainted in some very unexpected places—in the Tokyo airport, in hotels and motels, in churches, at his church's denominational headquarters.

"I was in bed most of the time," he wrote, "depressed and feeling like a pile of junk."

Doctors advised him, *"Leave the ministry!"*

His mother-in-law, Mrs. Choi, had a better idea. Instead, she mobilized a "Save the Pastor" campaign and enlisted hundreds of Koreans to pray for Dr. Cho. The woman served as the "spark plug" to recruit people who would help her plant a prayer hedge around this great man of God.

It worked! Dr. Cho was healed, and his life and message were kept intact. Even today, a carefully maintained prayer hedge protects Pastor Cho. He credits it with enabling him to become one of the most widely used men of God in the world today.[1]

Prayer hedges do work!

Satan would have loved for Dr. Cho to leave the ministry and sell automobiles or soap. Instead, through a wonderful woman of God, a pastor's ministry was spared—and Dr. Cho continued building the Full Gospel Central Church. Today, his church has grown to *700,000 members!*

The most successful pastors have behind them an entire army of quiet, consistently praying saints who make the difference. As a layperson, you can be the "spark plug" needed to ignite your church to pray for your shepherd before he or she is in crisis.

Mrs. Choi started a prayer emphasis that made all the difference. Only in heaven will we

know the complete story of how great a difference is made by faithful intercessors like Mrs.
Choi.

The Pastor's Professional Life

Have *you* ever been falsely accused?

One day, as some fellow pastors and I were
gathering for our weekly prayer meeting, we were
joined by the chaplain of one of this country's
largest Veterans' Administration hospitals.

"I'm devastated," he told us. "A nurse has
charged me with sexual harassment, and I am
totally innocent." With this pronouncement
made, he buried his face in his hands and
started to cry.

We knew the chaplain to be a person of un-
questionable integrity. He had prayed with many
people that they might receive Christ. So, we did
the only thing we knew to do. We gathered close
around him, prayed for him and made personal
commitments to continue lifting him up in prayer
until our next meeting.

Two weeks later, he came in smiling. The
chaplain told us how the hospital administrator
confronted the nurse, and she admitted to lying.
She was out to destroy his good name because
she envied his popularity. The nurse apologized,
and he forgave her.

With tears in his eyes, he thanked us for our
prayers. We had placed our shields of prayer over
him, and God protected him. His ministry was
spared from the darts of false accusation.

Stay constantly on guard. The forces of darkness will shoot accusations, but when there is a

prayer shield around the pastor, the lies and half-truths will be deflected. Is your pastor's professional life shielded?

The Pastor's Preaching Life

"How important is prayer to your pastor?"

Ask that question to Dr. Charles Stanley, and you will learn just how far prayer support can take a pastor of modest beginnings. Today, he is pastor of First Baptist Church, Atlanta, Georgia. Each Sunday, millions hear him preach the Word of God on radio and television. His speaking engagements are filled for years to come, and his writings are best-sellers in Christian bookstores coast to coast.

To Dr. Stanley, intercessory prayer is *very* important.

In his book, *How to Start a Prayer Group and Keep it Growing,* he writes,

> I have begun prayer groups in every church I have pastored. The members of these groups have often become my dearest friends, my most loyal supporters, and my most available resource for immediate help. I have felt them lifting me up on the Lord's day as I have stood to preach. They have prayed me through periods of discouragement and difficulty. A pastor can have no greater asset in his ministry than the faithful, consistent, fervent prayers of his people. When a pastor takes time to help a beginning prayer group or offer new life to one that needs a spark, he is light-

ing the fire to greater spiritual power in his own ministry.[2]

When you trace the history of Wesley, Spurgeon, Moody and other preachers who are today regarded as spiritual giants, you will inevitably find groups of intercessors who held up their hands with prayer while they preached.

Here's a thought. The next time you are traveling through Illinois, drive to Wheaton and visit the Billy Graham Center. You will see a magnificently displayed picture of Pearl Goode—Dr. Graham's most faithful intercessor.

All it takes is *one* person with enough faith to act!

Bill Dornbush knows the power of prayer. As pastor of First Presbyterian Church in Lapeer, Michigan, he says that knowing people are praying for him is a great encouragement for him to go on.

"Their prayers give me confidence that I can accomplish God's purposes," he says. "Ephesians 6:10-20 becomes a greater reality for me because I know I am not in the trenches standing alone against the enemy, but I have people guarding my backside as I move forward."

His prayer group bolsters the young pastor's courage.

"Knowing that people are praying for me also encourages me to become bold as I should be in proclaiming the gospel," Bill said. "With my prayer hedge, I sense a greater presence of God's Spirit directing me with a firm hand in personal and ministerial decisions."

It's also comforting for the pastor to know that his family is guarded by intercessory prayer as well. "I truly thank God for this unique partnership that supports my work through prayer," he said. "It's a wonderful feeling, knowing that your people are praying for you!"

Isn't that the kind of feeling every pastor should have? As a layperson, begin to pray for your pastor's messages as he or she preaches and see what happens. You will be pleasantly surprised.

The Pastor's Persevering Life

Poison arrows!! That's what welcomed Bruce Olson when he entered the land of the Motilone Indians in Columbia, South America. Most missionaries would have turned and fled, but not Bruce. He persevered and eventually won the entire tribe to Jesus Christ. He also helped them build schools and clinics.

Unfortunately, not everyone appreciated Bruce's work. In 1989, he was captured by political terrorists and held for nine months. During that time, he witnessed the murder of six fellow hostages. Once, his captors placed him in front of a firing squad and shot blanks to frighten him.

While preparing to die, he prayed for his captors. He was finally released, unharmed. One of his first acts after gaining his freedom was to write an open letter to the thousands of intercessors around the world who had been praying for his safe return.

"Your prayers had a profound effect," he wrote. "God heard and answered your petitions for me, for the Motilones, and even for my captors. The guerrillas may have believed in the beginning that it was they who controlled my fate, but in the end, more than sixty percent of my captors accepted the redeeming grace of Jesus Christ. They gladly attended the jungle schools I extemporaneously organized for them, where they learned to read and write and studied political and social sciences. I even taught them to cook—new ways with jungle cuisine! (Palm grubs and monkey entrails became their favorites.) As months passed, more and more guerrillas worshiped with me on Sundays. When I was close to death from intestinal hemorrhaging, guerrillas vied for the 'honor' of donating their blood to save me. When I was near death on several occasions they wept for me and even risked their own lives by showing their sympathy for me."

Bruce was subjected to threats on his life that are too gruesome for most of us to comprehend. It is only right that we recognize him as a modern day Paul. Not only did Bruce Olson persevere, he was enabled to be blessed with fruit for the kingdom in his adverse circumstances.

One of the greatest examples of prayer hedges comes from the life of Paul, who knew well the perils of being a New Testament pastor. Because of prayer, Paul persevered through some of the most horrible conditions imaginable. He was persecuted endlessly with threats to his life, continuous false accusations, troubles, hardships and distresses, beatings, imprisonments and riots, hard work, sleepless nights and hunger. He was dishonored and treated as an imposter, endured bad reports, was sorrowful, and lived without. He was deserted by fellow believers; he was mired in controversy. Paul worked another job while he preached and he faced the sentence of death. He was without a home or a family. He was tempted. He was shipwrecked and snake bit. He sat in prisons and worried over churches. I believe it was prayer that enabled him to fight the good fight, to finish the race and to keep the faith.

> *[Paul] was tempted. He was shipwrecked and snake bit. He sat in prisons and worried over churches.*

Paul wrote, "I am greatly encouraged; in all our troubles my joy knows no bounds" (2 Corinthians 7:4). On his departure, he told the young Timothy,

> You, however, know all about my teaching, my way of life, my purpose, faith, patience, love, endurance, persecutions, sufferings—what kind of things happened to me in Antioch, Iconium and Lystra, the persecutions I endured. Yet the Lord rescued me from all of them. . . . Preach the Word. . . (2 Timothy 3:10-11, 4:2).

Do what I did and expect the same! Amazing! What amazing grace that is. Why did Paul finish this obstacle course? He had a great God and a host of people praying for him. He finished the course because those on the sidelines cheered him on in prayer. Pastors need prayer to complete what they are called to do.

Pray for your shepherd to finish his or her course. Pray for endurance and final victory.

Plant a hedge, nurture it and water it, trim it in love, prop it up to grow strong and tall around your pastor. This will advance the kingdom of God, and the cause of Jesus Christ in the shepherd's life will flourish.

Chapter Five

Sheep Can Bite!

Do you know someone who could best be described as "violent," "cunning," "subtle," and "crafty?" The pastor of Green Acres Baptist Church in Houston can identify *six* people who match that description—and they all joined his church on the same Sunday morning. These people are masters of deceit. And, they were committed to *destroying* his church!

Granted, it sounds bizarre.

Reverend Jerry Goodguy never suspected a thing. Had he not dropped by the church late one evening to pick up a book, he might still be in the dark. When he heard a noise in the sanctuary, he stepped quietly inside to see what was happening.

What a surprise! His six new members were standing in a circle at the altar—holding a satanic "ritual" directed at the pastor. When he questioned them, they readily admitted their membership in a satanic cult, and that they were on a mission to undermine his ministry and devastate his church. The story is true.

Every pastor wants to lead his or her church to take their city for God. Pastors are at war with the forces of evil that are out to destroy them. The enemy is a liar and can disguise himself as an angel of light. His weapons of destruction are darts of distrust, skepticism, disunity, seduction, coercion, depression, self-doubt and disaster.

> *Pastors are at war with the forces of evil that are out to destroy them.*

Satan is the antithesis of everything Jesus Christ stands for. Pray that you and your pastor will have the insight to recognize the sheep that are intent on biting their shepherd. Read Ephesians 6. Paul lists the full armor of God as a source of protection and blessing. Use this passage to pray over your pastor as he or she does battle with the enemy. Use prayer to protect your church and its pastor.

Most New Testament-inspired paintings of sheep are rather idyllic. You have a shepherd overlooking some white, fluffy, lovable lambs. Remember the scene of a shepherd carrying a little lamb on his shoulders while the other sheep gaze up at him with an "isn't that nice" look in their eyes? However, Dr. Mark Rutland reminds us that sheep can bite. In fact, they can knock you down, stomp on you and drag you into the bushes for dead.

If you have ever pastored a flock, you know this to be true. Just move their table, bring a guitar into the sanctuary or change the order of the service, and they come at you with teeth flashing and fire in their eyes! You can go to any denominational preachers' meeting and listen to the pastors, and they will show you the scars and teeth marks left by irate sheep.

The Perils of Pastoring

Have you ever seen pettiness threaten the life of a church?

My Mexican-American friend, Carlos, is pastor of a small church overlooking the Rio Grande. I have a special place in my heart for Carlos and his burden for ministering to people who have disabilities. On Sunday mornings, he often encourages parents to bring their children with physical or mental disabilities into the worship service. "All of these children belong to our Heavenly Father," Carlos explains. "It is only right that they, too, be allowed to worship with us."

One morning as Carlos was preaching, a 12-year-old boy who had mental retardation jumped up from his pew and ran to the front of the church. For the remainder of the service, he stood alongside the pastor with a big grin on his face.

Some of the members were visibly upset. As one layman was leaving the worship service, he expressed his displeasure to Carlos. "That boy disrupted our entire service," the man said. "We should not tolerate such behavior in the House of God." Others were quick to agree.

When Carlos saw their reaction, he became angry and admonished their intolerance toward one of God's children. The following week, instead of receiving affirmation for his special ministry to persons with disabilities, Carlos was forced to deal with what he soon learned was a well-organized telephone campaign of naysayers who were adamantly opposed to him.

Carlos felt hurt and betrayed by the flock he was trying to serve. He learned a painful lesson. Unless a pastor has a good prayer hedge, the opposition can gain a lot of ground very quickly. What Carlos needed, before the trouble ever started brewing, was a prayer hedge made up of those who favored his special ministry to persons with handicapping conditions.

Don't wait until the enemy is coming over the horizon leading a battle charge against your pastor. *Now* is the time to build a hedge that will become a strong defense. It will enable your shepherd to withstand the pettiness that often plagues ministry. Start praying for your pastor today, lest he or she be preyed on.

The New Testament is certainly clear about the perils of pastoring. Yet it is amazing how we neglect to study these teachings. Instead we focus on things we find easier to understand, such as the qualifications for church leadership and the requirements of personal holiness.

The book of Acts abounds with examples of church leadership being both attacked and blessed under the pressure of a growing ministry. Paul states, "I only know that in every city the Holy Spirit warns me that prison and hardships are facing me" (Acts 20:23). In 2 Corinthians 6:4-10, he adds,

Rather, as servants of God we commend ourselves in every way: in great endurance; . . . in beatings, imprisonments and riots; in hard work, sleepless nights and hunger; in purity, understanding, patience and kindness; in the Holy Spirit and in sincere love; in truthful speech and in the power of God; with weapons of righteousness in the right hand and in the left; through glory and dishonor, bad report and good report; genuine, yet regarded as impostors; . . . dying and yet we live on; beaten, and yet not killed; sorrowful, yet always rejoicing; poor, yet making many rich; having nothing and yet possessing everything.

Here Paul parallels the blessings with the hardships, the qualifications with the pressures of shepherding, the good with the bad. It is no easy road to be a pastor at any time in any place. Any view of leadership that neglects the consequences of being a pastor is a truncated model. If there were no perils, pressures or persecutions, prayer would not be needed. The Bible teaches—and even guarantees—pressures and problems with the blessings in pastoring. Therefore, a protective prayer hedge for the pastor is essential.

A Clash of Kingdoms

"Please *cancel* the prayer seminar." That's the request of a letter I received concerning a scheduled prayer seminar in south Alabama that I wanted very much to conduct. "I can't handle it," the pastor wrote.

I read on. "Prior to the Aldersgate Conference in '92 I was preaching on the person and work of the Holy Spirit. I returned home from our meeting more determined than ever to preach for the renewal of the church," he said. Then, he dropped the bombshell.

"What I managed to do was stir up both that which is wonderful and that which is both ugly and painful. It is not the time for a prayer conference. I have much opposition to it. My future here is uncertain and I must be sensitive to God's backing one day at a time. I covet your prayers and trust that you understand my need to cancel."

Sure, I can read between the lines. It was the proverbial "clash of kingdoms" that every pastor learns to work around—or he or she no longer has a church to pastor! What else could he have done?

The New Testament mandate to pray for the pastor is necessary for a very good reason: *The gospel is confrontational.* It was then, and it is now. The gospel of Jesus continually calls people to new life, new convictions, new power, a new fruitfulness, a new set of values, a new way of looking at people and a new freedom. Jesus calls us to leave the old and cling to the new. He was the one who gave a us a new commandment. He brought a new covenant. He offers a new life and a new way. In Revelation 21:5, Jesus said, "I am making everything new!" The gospel is always the *new* movement of God, and pastors are the heralds of this new move.

The gospel confronts sin and beckons repentance and holiness, and it is planted in us to bear new fruit. Paul writes to the Colossians, "All over the world this gospel is producing fruit and growing, just as it has been doing among you since the day you heard it and understood God's grace in all its truth" (1:6).

John Ogilvie, pastor of the First Presbyterian Church in Hollywood, reminds us in one of his sermons that, "There is nothing same, lame or tame about the gospel."

In addition to being confrontational, the gospel also promotes a clash of kingdoms. Dudley Hall reminds us in his book *Out of the Comfort Zone* that the people of the old move of God can fight or resist the people of the new move of God.[1]

History bears witness to this principle again and again. The new reign and rule of Jesus Christ clashed with the old reign of sin and religion. The gospel of light clashes with the kingdom of darkness. Quite often the pastor gets caught in the clash and is crushed in between the old move and the new move.

Blessed and Battered: A Look at the Book of Acts

An overview of the New Testament reveals that pastors are blessed and battered: Hands are "laid on" to ordain, and they are "laid on" to kill.

Paul writes in his first letter to the Corinthians, "But I will stay on at Ephesus until Pentecost, because a great door for effective work has opened to me [the new move of God], and there are many who oppose me" (16:8-9). Therefore, he admonishes them, "Be on your guard, stand firm in the faith; be men of courage; be strong" (16:13). The book of Acts is especially useful for understanding the perils of pastoring, as well as the pressures of bearing new fruit in the kingdom of God.

Changed Lives and Death Threats

A changed life is an indictment of an unchanged life and pastors are often blamed for the change!

In Acts 16, a young slave girl is delivered and saved. Her life is completely changed. As a result, her owners see no hope of making any more money using her. They seize the pastors and drag them into the market place. There they are stripped, beaten severely and cast into prison!

There are at least six other instances in Acts where pastors are put in prison for preaching. Such are the results of preaching about a life-changing Savior.

It is estimated that in the first five chapters of Acts, more than 20,000 people came to the Lord. Can you imagine a pastor just trying to get these names written on the official roll? Just think about ordering children's literature for all these new families. In almost every chapter lives are changed by Jesus Christ. People fall under conviction, repent and are baptized. The pastors are blessed and the church expands. However, for every person who does repent, there are many who fight this new truth about Jesus and the need to repent.

In Acts 9, Paul is radically changed on the road to Damascus. He receives a new life in Christ, and he immediately begins to testify to Jesus. He grows more and more powerful in bearing witness. Then we read in verse 23, "After many days had gone by, the Jews conspired to kill him . . ." This new pastor was in deep trouble! The old order did not buy his new message and new life. Their solution was to kill him! But Paul became a "basket case," and escaped through a hole in the wall (verse 25). His new life had not reflected favorably upon the lives of those who had rejected the gospel.

The Tensions of New Convictions

The Acts of the Apostles also reveal the tensions caused by the new and bold convictions of Jesus Christ. Jesus calls us to believe in a new way, and sometimes even cherished doctrines must be confronted and called to change.

For example, in Christ, we believe new things about ourselves, God, and others. In Acts 4:2-4, many people heard and believed the message Peter and John were preaching and "the number of men grew to about five thousand." As a result, the Jews were "greatly disturbed," and they "seized Peter and John," threatening them to cease teaching this new doctrine.

The same was true in Acts 6 and 7, when Pastor Stephen preached a new conviction which called for receiving Jesus Christ as the Messiah. They seized him, and brought him before the Sanhedrin. When they heard this pastor's convictions, "they were furious and gnashed their teeth at him," and they all "rushed at him, dragged him out of the city and began to stone him" (Acts 7:54, 57-58).

In Acts 13, we see another example of the clash between the old and new thanks to Pastor Paul and Pastor Barnabas. They preached a new doctrine that the Gentiles could be saved, and many believed. We read, "When the Gentiles heard this, they were glad and honored the word of the Lord; and all who were appointed for eternal life believed. The word of the Lord spread through the whole region" (Acts 13:48-49). Some people, however, refused to change their convictions (verse 50): "But the Jews incited the God-fearing women of high standing and the leading men of the city. They stirred up persecution against Paul and Barnabas," and had them moved to another church!

Paul and Barnabas, like Peter, John and Stephen, got into trouble because of what they believed. When the Prince of all principles beckons us to a new conviction, the end result can be conflict for those who teach and follow Jesus Christ.

Revival and Riots

A third source of opposition to pastors that we see in the book of Acts is the new power released in believers through the Holy Spirit. Pastors can get in trouble by being "too spiritual." As the pastors in Acts proclaimed the powerful name of Jesus, signs and wonders followed their preaching. With this new power, they preached the Word and healed the sick.

Acts 14:3 tells us that Paul and Barnabas spoke "boldly for the Lord, who confirmed the message of his grace by enabling them to do miraculous signs and wonders." The end result was, "the Jews who refused to believe stirred up the Gentiles and poisoned their minds against the brothers [pastors] . . .the people of the city were divided . . . . There was a plot . . . to mistreat them and stone them" (Acts 14:2, 4-5).

The same thing happened in Lystra. A man was healed and "some Jews came from Antioch and Iconium and won the crowd over. They stoned Paul and dragged him outside the city, thinking he was dead" (Acts 14:19). Your pastor can get into trouble for praying for people in Jesus' name, especially when people are healed! A dead church is indicted by an alive church. The supernatural can upset a church whose norm is the natural. It is appropriate that the King James Version of the Bible calls the Holy Spirit the "Holy Ghost," for he tends to haunt a church that is trying to do things in their own strength!

Pastors who operate in the "safe zone" rarely get in trouble. It is the name of Jesus that causes a stir one way or the other. That is why in Acts 4:18 the rulers, elders and teachers called the pastors in and "commanded them not to speak or teach at all in the name of Jesus."

Jealous Jews

Jesus said in John 15:8, "This is to my Father's glory, that you bear much fruit, showing yourselves to be my disciples." This fruit provided another source of conflict for pastors in Acts, because the blessings caused by the gospel made the Jews jealous.

In Acts 5:16 we read, "Crowds gathered also from the towns around Jerusalem, bringing their sick and those tormented by evil spirits, and all of them were healed." As a result, "the high priest and all his associates . . . were filled with jealousy. They arrested the apostles [pastors] and put them in the public jail" (Acts 5:17-18). Later in Acts 13:44-45 we read, "On the next Sabbath almost the whole city gathered to hear the word of the Lord. When the Jews saw the crowds, they were filled with jealously and talked abusively against what Paul was saying." When the Jews saw the blessings that resulted from the gospel, they were indignant because the fruit of the gospel indicted their own lack of results. As the Word began to spread through the whole region, the Jews felt so threatened that they "stirred up persecution against Paul and Barnabas and expelled them from their region" (Acts 13:50).

These pastors got into trouble as the church grew and became a dynamic influence in the community. But that is not the end of the story. Paul moved to Thessalonica, where some of the Jews were persuaded to join Paul and Silas, "as did a large number of God-fearing Greeks and not a few prominent women" (Acts 17:4).

Again, the gospel produced results, and as before, "the Jews were jealous; so they rounded up some bad characters from the marketplace, formed a mob and started a riot in the city" (Acts 17:5). So Paul moved again, eventually coming to Corinth, where Crispus, the synagogue ruler, believed along with many Corinthians (Acts 18:8). The consequences were the same. The Jews made yet another united attack on Paul (Acts 19:12) as a result of the blessings that were poured out when he preached Jesus Christ.

The gospel *is* confrontational. Where Jesus is preached, things happen: revival and riots and jealousy. Jesus said, "This is to my Father's glory, that you bear much fruit. . . ." The New Testament pastors learned that a growing, dynamic church that is blessed with much fruit will cause opposition and jealously to arise. Often the attack will be aimed at the leader—the pastor.

Let's Accuse a Pastor!

Finally, the pastors in the New Testament came under attack from a spirit of accusation. The gospel they were preaching called men and women to a new and bold affirmation. In Christ, people are commended before God based on the righteousness of Jesus and affirmed as being set free from the Law.

In Christ, people are declared forgiven, redeemed and healed. They are under grace: ". . . if anyone is in Christ, he is a new creation; the old has gone, the new has come!" (2 Corinthians 5:17). For the law-lovers, this was not good news. They radically opposed this new teaching of grace. Often, the thrust of their attack was that of accusation.

The pastors in Acts were constantly being accused. In Acts 6, Stephen is accused by the teachers of the Law of "speaking against" their holy place, the synagogue, and against the Law. Because "they could not stand up against his wisdom or the Spirit by which he spoke," they had to secretly persuade some men to bring this accusation by using false witness.

In Acts 16, Paul and Silas were accused of starting a riot in the city by advocating customs unlawful for the Romans to practice. The very ones who brought the accusation were those who started the riot!

Later in Acts 19, Paul was accused of under-mining the temple of the goddess Artemis. A sil-versmith, who made a good income by building shrines for the temple, convinced his men that Paul was not only a threat to their financial suc-cess, but that he also was discrediting the god-dess. The men became furious. Then in chapter 21, Pastor Paul, like Stephen, was accused of defiling the Holy Place and he was arrested.

Acts 25:7 reveals the force and energy of the accusations against Paul: "When Paul appeared, the Jews who had come down from Jerusalem stood around him, bringing many serious charges against him, which they could not prove."

It is little wonder that Revelation 12:10 refers to Satan as "the accuser of our brothers." Ev-erywhere Paul went, the religious leaders joined in the accusations. The gospel affirms and com-mends us in truth, but the liar accuses and pulls down the pastor.

Because the world thrives on rumors and half-truths, accusation is one of the most lethal weapons that can be used against a pastor.

Yesterday, Today and Forever

Clearly, it was not easy being a New Testament pastor. In addition to the attacks listed above, the New Testament describes other difficulties that pastors went through. Paul was ship-wrecked and snake-bit. He went without food and suffered an assortment of attacks on his life and ministry. James, the brother of John, was killed by Herod. John was exiled to the Island of Patmos. The perils of New Testament leadership were as real as the blessings.

For pastors today the risks of pastoring have not changed because the gospel has not changed. Hebrews 13:7 says, "Jesus Christ is the same yesterday and today and forever." If a pastor today preaches Jesus in all his fullness, majesty and truth, the results will be the same. Lives will be changed. New convictions will replace old, dead beliefs. Jesus will baptize people in new power and authority. New fruit will burst forth in churches. As the kingdom of God is blessed for preaching Jesus, pastors will face all kinds of accusations, threats and jealousy from those who do not believe.

There will always be opposition to a pastor who preaches Jesus as the best way, the only way and the way to God.

What's Going on Here?

When we read about the violent reaction to these New Testament pastors, we wonder, "What was really going on here?"

These were vagabond preachers with no reputation, no money, no education, no weapons and no tangible literature to distribute. They were men from the lower classes of life—fisherman, former tax collectors, laborers. These ragtag pastors preached a scandalous message about a convicted criminal who died on the cross by a garbage heap! They said he was alive, having been raised from the dead, and that he was going to come back in the clouds to get those who believed in him. They claimed miracles in his name and said that he forgave sin. They even taught people to give to the poor and sell their property if necessary. How astounding!

Yet even more astounding was the reaction of the "officials" to these pastors. They put them in jail, beat them, exiled them and even killed them. Normally, the Jews and the Romans hated each other, but when it came to the Christians, they collaborated to get rid of them.

> **Normally, the Jews and the Romans hated each other, but when it came to the Christians, they collaborated to get rid of them.**

In a world of constant religious debate and controversy, the Christians were always in the middle. Stephen was stoned because the people overreacted to his sermon. Later, James would be executed and Peter was arrested to be killed. How's that for disagreement?

Of course, Paul seemed to attract more attention than anyone. When he defected to the Christian ranks, the Jews conspired against him several times. At one time, 40 Jews vowed to sit on the side of the road just to wait for the opportunity to attack him, and later a whole flock of Jewish leaders and high-powered lawyers followed him around, all trying to get him killed. In Acts 25:2, the chief priests even went to the Roman governor, Festus, to try to get Paul.

Paul was beaten, stoned and left for dead, then sent all the way to Rome for trial. How amazing that one man could get so much attention from a whole nation of leaders—and all for preaching Jesus.

All of these New Testament pastors simply preached love and forgiveness, and everywhere they went there were riots and mob responses.

In Acts 19 they were accused of undermining the temple of the goddess Artemis, a national cult that worshiped in Colosse, Laodicea and throughout Asia. Were these few, itinerate preachers really a threat to undo this widespread cult? Were they capable of destroying her magnificence? What was *really* going on?

Paul had the answer in Ephesians 6:12:

> For our struggle is not against flesh and blood, but against the rulers, against the authorities, against the powers of this dark world and against the spiritual forces of evil in the heavenly realms.

These pastors faced resistance not for political, economic or religious reasons. Rather, they were engaged in spiritual warfare. Behind the worldly scene of riots and angry religious officials were the unseen forces of Satan. The followers of Christ wanted to deliver captives from the kingdom of darkness into the kingdom of light. As Mark Rutland so correctly asks, "The real question here is, 'Who is in charge?'"

I know a man named Jeff who pastors a small church in Vermont where he preaches one service on Sunday morning. He told me that he dreads preaching in this church because after the service he is totally drained. He eats lunch and then falls in bed for three to four hours! He wakes up feeling like a train ran over him.

Jeff wonders why it is so hard to preach to 40 people. Before coming to this church, he loved preaching. Could a spiritual resistance be draining him?

Satan does not want people to be saved. Salvation glorifies God and Satan hates for God to be glorified. Anything that prevents people from being saved—today as in New Testament times—Satan promotes.

C. Peter Wagner, in his book *Warfare Prayer*, writes,

> Jesus came to seek and save the lost. God sent his Son that whosoever believes in him should have everlasting life. Whensoever a person is saved the angels in heaven rejoice. Satan hates all the above. He wants people to go to hell, not to heaven. And the reason this is his primary objective is that each time he succeeds he has won an eternal victory.[2]

Have you ever met a witch?

Dr. Paul Walker, pastor of Mt. Perrin Church of God, was flying back to Atlanta. He sat next to a woman who refused the flight meal. He asked, "Are you a fasting Christian?"

She replied, "No, I am a witch, and the covens of Atlanta are praying for the breakup of the marriages of Charles Stanley, Paul Walker and Mark Rutland."

Naturally, Dr. Walker did not tell her who he was.

In essence there are territorial spirits assigned over cities and other specific areas to haunt the preaching of the gospel, and they fight constantly in whatever way possible to prevent pastors and churches from winning the lost.

The Pastor Sets the Pace

As the leaders in our mission to take cities for Jesus Christ, pastors are the point men. They take the direct fire. As a pastor to other pastors, I know this to be the case today. Anything that helps people come to Christ, these evil spirits oppose. Let me share an example.

One of my goals is to help churches build prayer rooms where people can come regularly to intercede for their community or for needs in their church. We hope to have 1,000 prayer rooms in place by the year 2,000 to facilitate the salvation of cities.

I have written about this in my book, *Making Room to Pray*.[3] The purpose is to soak a city and a church in prayer and give the Holy Spirit control to dispatch angels to push back the power of darkness. When this happens the church can reap a harvest—and the enemy hates this!

One pastor in Virginia Beach, South Carolina put a prayer room in his church, and then discovered that one of his members adamantly opposed it. On Palm Sunday, this woman took the microphone without permission and said, "I oppose this prayer room idea for the following reasons: If we use the proposed room we'll have nowhere to put the hand bells; my sister will have nowhere to hang her organ robe; someone might trip getting into the prayer room; and, someone might get raped in there."

The congregation began to laugh until they realized she was serious. She and her family left the church and are conducting a phone campaign to oust the pastor.

In Richland, Indiana, a pastor got excited during his sermon one morning and jumped up and down and came out from behind the pulpit. The next week he was called on the carpet. Five "controllers" told him, "We do not have shows of enthusiasm like that in our church, and our preachers stay behind the pulpit."

Another friend, after lifting the offering plates up over the altar one Sunday, was told he was being too dramatic. A pastor in Phoenix was given a list of people *not* to visit, lest they come to church. A pastor in East Texas was accused of having a hobby that cost too much. I have sat in board meetings with a sick feeling in my stomach watching power struggles over what kind of candles to buy. Does any of this make sense?

The enemy majors in pettiness to keep pastors drained and distracted from the real issue of taking their cities for God. The question pastors face when they desire revival is, "Who's in charge here?" The issues causing much pain to pastors are really not the color of the carpet or which hymnal to use—the issues are spiritual. We are in a spiritual battle.

Satan hates pastors because they are the visible leaders. They are the ranking officers of local movements to win the lost. They were the target in Acts and they are the target now.

Let me ask you, how many pastors can you count who have fallen by the wayside in the last several years? And I'm not just talking about TV evangelists. I'm talking about local pastors.

Right now one of the most embarrassing problems in the Catholic Church is priests being accused of molesting children. My own conference has seen one painful divorce after another over infidelity. One large church in Atlanta that seats 7,700 people has just been rocked by multiple affairs in the church staff.

A recent article in *Ministries Today* by attorney and CPA Richard Hammar says, "In recent years we've heard an increasing number of reports about pastors, priests, and other clergy members who have been found guilty of sexually exploiting victims in counseling sessions." Hammar explains that the courts are taking sexual contact between ministers and those they counsel very seriously, even when the contact is consensual. He says that four states have already passed laws making this contact a crime, five states are considering similar legislation and many more will undoubtedly do so in the near future. He adds, "Wise pastors, ministers and church leaders will become familiar with the contents of these statutes."[4]

It takes churches years to recover momentum after an adulterous scandal. The issues of pain, accusation and sin are not matters of just poor choice or burnout or policy changes. They are often the evidence of controlling spirits on assignment to destroy or neutralize a dynamic local pastor who has a vision and a zeal for souls.

Peter Wagner wisely observes,

> We often fail to recognize the depth of the spiritual battle we are fighting. The enemy knows pastors are beat up, he knows they are vulnerable, and he attacks them at

their weakest point. This is not to say that these who have fallen are not themselves guilty and do not have character flaws that need to be repaired through humility, repentance, reconciliation, restoration, and holiness. But I do hope and pray we will learn how to use our spiritual weapons more effectively in putting a stop to these blatant and all too successful attacks of the devil.[5]

New Testament Prayer and Pastors

It is little wonder that Jesus prayed on the eve of his departure for his pastors. In John 17:9, 11 and 15 he said, "I pray for them . . . Holy Father, protect them by the power of your Name—the Name you gave me—so that they may be one as we are one. . . . My prayer is not that you take them out of the world but that you protect them from the evil one." Jesus also warned his followers, "If the world hates you, keep in mind that it hated me first," and, "If they persecuted me, they will persecute you also" (John 15:18, 20). He told them they would have tribulation.

If Jesus believed this, we should. If he prayed for the pastors, we should. In the New Testament, Jesus modeled prayer for pastors. The churches of the New Testament followed his example—they prayed consistently for their pastors! It was taken for granted to pray for Pastor John or Paul.

Today, the pastor is often just taken for granted. In the early church, a strong prayer life was so prevalent and important that churches did not have to be told to pray. If they did not, they simply ceased to be. Read through the verses of Thessalonians and you will find a church that "prayed without ceasing," for in reality, they had little to distract them from personal and corporate prayer. They had no building program, no choir practice, no Bible studies (they had no NIV Bible!), no policy or budget meetings, no annual convention. They just met in homes, orally adhered to the apostles' teaching, broke bread together, enjoyed fellowship and prayed. The leadership lived and ministered in an atmosphere of prayer.

Nothing ever started in the New Testament without prayer, including the pastors' ministries. They were bathed in it. Pastors were prayed for from the very start. Pastor Paul got his start in ministry when Ananias laid hands on him and he was filled with the Holy Spirit. In Acts 14:23, Paul and Barnabas chose pastors for each church and then fasted and prayed and committed themselves to the Lord. Before Peter preached on the Day of Pentecost, the apostles met in the Upper Room and had a prayer meeting where the Holy Spirit was invoked. Peter's preaching was empowered by the saints in the Upper Room. This church knew how to pray for its preachers! Paul could say with confidence,

> Pray also for me, that whenever I open my mouth, words may be given me so that I will fearlessly make known the mystery of the gospel. . . . Pray that I may declare it fearlessly, as I should (Ephesians 6:19-20).

A prayed-for pastor is an anointed preacher!

The early church also met to pray whenever their pastors were in danger. In Acts 4, Peter and John had been threatened not to preach the name of Jesus. So the people prayed. "After they prayed, the place where they were meeting was shaken. They were all filled with the Holy Spirit and spoke the word of God boldly" Acts 4:31).

These pastors did not face threats alone. When the pastors were arrested and their lives endangered, the early church prayed to rescue them. In Acts 12:5 we read, "So Peter was kept in prison, but the church was earnestly praying to God for him." Then, as the story goes, an angel was sent to set Peter free. Someone has said, "The angel fetched Peter, but it was prayer that fetched the angel!"

Paul was quick to ask the church to pray for him, saying,

> I urge you, brothers, by our Lord Jesus Christ and by the love of the Spirit, to join me in my struggle by praying to God for me. Pray that I may be rescued from the unbelievers in Judea . . . (Romans 15:30).

Evidently the early church did pray for Paul, because he was rescued innumerable times. In fact, he once remarked,

> He has delivered us from such a deadly peril, and he will deliver us. On him we have set our hope that he will continue to deliver us, as you help us by your prayers. Then many will give thanks on our behalf for the gracious favor granted us in answer to the prayers of many (2 Corinthians 1:10-11).

Prayer from the church not only reinforced these pastors in the face of spiritual opposition, but at times it literally saved their lives.

The church also prayed for the people to receive their pastors' messages and for doors of opportunity to open. Again, Paul exhorted the church, "Devote yourselves to prayer, being watchful and thankful. And pray for us, too, that God may open a door for our message . . ." (Colossians 4:2-3). And God did open that door—again and again. When the church prayed, the pastors received direction, churches were planted and whole regions were evangelized. A good example of this is in Acts 13 when Barnabas and Paul were set apart for their first missionary journey. The church was worshiping the Lord and fasting. They laid hands on their pastors and prayed for them and for the success of the mission. They became a part of their pastors' ministry by praying and fasting for open doors of opportunity.

Prayer was also offered to bring closure to a pastor's ministry. In Acts 20:17-38, Pastor Paul said good-bye to the church at Ephesus and he knelt down with all of them and prayed. Pastors were prayed for both coming and going!

One of the most touching scenes in the book of Acts demonstrates how highly committed the early church was to its pastors, and the power of prayer that resulted from their devotion. In Acts 14:19-20, Pastor Paul had preached in Lystra and had healed a lame man. The Jews became so angry that they came from Antioch, formed a mob and dragged Paul outside the city where they stoned him and left him for dead.

Imagine the grief the disciples must have felt as they gathered around their beaten and bloodied pastor. They must have wept over him and cried out to God. In the midst of this display, Paul "got up and went back into the city."

Wow! There he lay under a pile of stones—dead. But the church gathered around him and prayed, and God raised him up.

Persecutions Continue

The gospel has not changed. It is still the power of God unto the saving of souls. To preach the gospel is to call men and women and children to live a new life in Christ. To preach this gospel is to call people to live holy lives in a corrupt generation. As in the early church, the results will be the same. The kingdom will grow and persecutions will follow. As then, so now, the new order will confront the old order and there will be tension. If the enemy did not like the pastors then, the enemy will not like the pastors now. As they were attacked then, so they will be attacked now because we are still in a spiritual conflict. The types and kinds of attack may vary, but nevertheless they will continue.

The enemy knows the principle in Zechariah 13:7, "Strike the shepherd, and the sheep will be scattered." If the pastor falters, the church has a difficult time. In all probability, when there is no life in the pulpit, there will be no life in the pew. No passion for souls in the pulpit means no passion for souls in the pew.

The pastor sets the pace and vision for the local congregation. Knowing this, the enemy's aim is to strike the pastor with fear, accusations, family problems, financial setbacks, sickness, disease, depression, fear of others, lawsuits and so on. You name it, and he will throw it at pastors' private lives, personal family relationships, their prayer and praise lives, their professional confidence and their preaching. The enemy knows no detente. He is out to destroy pastors and their fruits.

A Personal Experience

We are at war with an unseen spiritual enemy who opposes pastors at every turn. I experienced great resistance in the writing of this book. Even as I wrote, I felt weak and headaches were frequent. I endured constant mental attacks. I went to bed often. In the middle of its writing, my mother died unexpectedly. I had to ask for constant prayer from my church.

When I gave the manuscript to my typist, she got sick and went to bed with eye problems. I gave it to a second typist, and when I called her to pray for her protection, she was at the emergency room with her son! Her computer even refused to work several times.

It is open season on pastors and the enemy does not want them prayed for. He wants to prey on them.

An Urgent Call to Pray

A prayer hedge is urgent and necessary. I believe this is one of the most serious issues facing the church today. As a layperson, you are the key to planting such a hedge around your shepherd.

Your pastor is important in your life. He or she feeds you the Word, teaches your children, gives you the sacraments and is with you in sorrow and death. Your pastor is there to represent Jesus Christ in your community.

Will you begin to raise up a prayer hedge in your church? Will you be the one to pray for your pastor like the early church did, with enough tenacity to save him or her from deadly peril? Will your pastor be preyed on or prayed for? It's up to *you!*

Over the years, as I have interacted with pastors across our nation, I have observed one common thread that ties them all together. Peter Wagner summed it up when he stated,

> Regardless of educational background, tenure, or denominational affiliation, relentless personal pressure is created from long hours of ministerial involvement in the lives of hurting and troubled people while at the same time being responsible for the disposition of their own family and the business of the church.[6]

Without a personal prayer life, a strong hedge of protection and the blessing which comes through the intercession of the congregation, a pastor stands little chance of long-term success. In all probability, the hands of pastors who are not prayed for will grow too tired, they will fall to their sides and the battle will be lost.

It is imperative that we, the church, rise to the challenge and begin to hedge in our pastors with our prayers.

Chapter Six

The Power of Prayer

Do you believe in a "sixth sense?" I used to be a skeptic, but no more!

One day, while my wife was at home washing dishes she suddenly felt a change taking place. It wasn't anything specific. Perhaps it was a slight variation in temperature, or an unexplainable quietness that—in a second or two—encompassed the space around her. Whatever the reason, she felt that the Holy Spirit had an immediate need to let her know that our oldest son, Travis, was dangerously close to loosing his life.

My wife quickly slipped off her apron, bowed her head, and opened her heart to God in prayer. From Psalms 91 and Luke 10:19 she knew God's promise of protection, and she prayed in Jesus' name in the Holy Spirit.

Travis was definitely in danger. As she prayed, our son was racing out of town at 120 miles per hour on a motorcycle that was, at best, unsafe. When he finally brought the bike to a stop, the back tire went completely flat.

God had answered my wife's prayers! Having ridden motorcycles in my younger years, I know that having a flat tire at 120 m.p.h. would have meant instant death. The thing that keeps coming back to me is how my wife was visited by the Holy Spirit, how quickly she responded and what a difference her prayers made in the future of a young man who was in real danger.

> *The most powerful weapon that day was not on the battlefield...*

One boy. One prayer. One life saved!

"Amazing," you say? Not really. Read the intriguing story documented in Exodus 17. Three men, armed only with prayer, turned the tide in the battle between the Israelites led by Joshua and the Amalekites.

Two armies, clad in armor, trained in battle, and led by generals faced off with each other. Swords clashed, chariots raced, men shouted and fell dead in the fury of hand-to-hand combat. Yet the victory was determined not by war strategies, but by three men on the mountain. As Moses prayed, and as Aaron and Hur lifted his hands, Joshua and his troops prevailed.

The most powerful weapon that day was not on the battlefield but on the mountaintop: it was prayer that enabled Joshua to overcome the Amalekite army with the sword. What a testimony to the power of prayer!

Covenant Prayer

You may not know Reinhard Bonnke. What's important is that hundreds of thousands of Africans *do* know him. Many of them know him personally as "The man who has claimed Africa for Jesus Christ." If you ask Bonnke, "Who is holding up your hands?" you'll get a quick reply: "Suzette Hattingh!"

Before the evangelist leaves home to lead a crusade, Suzette mobilizes thousands to offer intercessory prayers in a covenant with God to protect and bless this great spiritual leader in all he says and does. During the actual crusade, while Reinhard is preaching, Suzette and hundreds of others are kneeling in a nearby tent praying that the Holy Spirit will prevail.

"It's not a case of singing choruses and praying for a blessing, but of pulling down the strongholds of Satan," Bonnke said. Then she added, "Intercessors are a mighty battering ram!"[1]

Who should be praying for your pastor while he or she preaches?

The power of prayer itself is rooted in the Biblical concept of covenant. In planting a prayer hedge, it is important to understand this covenant theology, and why it is the basis for all prayer.

In Exodus 34:10, the Lord says to Moses,

> I am making a covenant with you. Before all your people I will do wonders never before done in any nation in all the world. The people you live among will see how awesome is the work that I, the LORD, will do for you.

The central idea in a covenant is commitment. God was promising in Exodus to commit himself to man in a redemptive process that man would reciprocate in a commitment to God.

The Hebrew word for covenant means "to cut until blood flows." This form of covenant was the most serious kind in the Old Testament. When men entered a blood covenant, it was for life. They exchanged coats as a symbol of their identities being merged. They gave weapons to vow protection for each other. They also exchanged names to give the other access to their own property and rights. Finally, they would cut their wrists, press them together, and let the life blood flow between them to symbolize the binding nature of the covenant. If the covenant was broken, death could be the penalty. Divorce was out of the question. Old Testament covenant was extremely serious.

Beginning with Noah, God would initiate a series of covenants with Abraham, Moses and David to reveal his love for us in a commitment that would culminate in the new covenant ratified by his son. The old covenant was but a shadow of a better one to come. Yet, in the old covenant, the principles of prayer are set in motion to be fulfilled in Jesus Christ.

A prayer hedge needs to be seen in the light and depth of covenant. Prayer is powerful because of the Lord's commitment to us and ours to him. Covenant prayer is the means of knowing God personally. Covenant prayer is also the vehicle for his interaction and provision in our lives. Through the new covenant, God invests himself in us to make us his peculiar people.

Let me explain. Covenant prayer teaches us that the purpose of prayer is not just to "get something" from God. It is a means of knowing God personally and intimately.

God wants us to be his people. He tells us,

I will take you as my own people, and I will be your God. Then you will know that I am the LORD your God. . . . Now if you obey me fully and keep my covenant, then out of all nations you will be my treasured possession. Although the whole earth is mine, you will be for me a kingdom of priests and a holy nation" (Exodus 6:7; 19:5).

Jesus said it like this,

As the Father has loved me, so have I loved you. Now remain in my love. If you obey my commands, you will remain in my love, just as I have obeyed my Father's commands and remain in his love. I have told you this so that my joy may be in you and that your joy may be complete. . . . I have called you friends, for everything that I learned from my Father I have made known to you (John 15:9-11, 15).

Prayer is the act of being bound in love to our God. Further, the Father seeks to display his glory and majesty in us. He wants to see us redeemed and victorious over our enemies. He desires to guide us and see his kingdom displayed in us, his people. As his splendor is displayed in us, his glory is manifest and the world will see and believe (John 2:11). In the idea of covenant, all that is his is ours, and all that is ours is his.

Prayer is the mysterious means by which we interact with our heavenly Father. It is the covenant vehicle for the people of God to receive his glory.

In both the old and new covenants, we see this dynamic. For example, Deuteronomy 4:29 says, "But if from there you seek the LORD your God, you will find him if you look for him with all your heart and with all your soul." This is the Old Testament basis for "calling" upon God in personal and corporate prayer. Jesus said,

> Ask and it will be given you; seek and you will find; knock and the door will be opened to you. For everyone who asks receives; he who seeks finds; and to him who knocks, the door will be opened.... how much more will your Father in heaven give good gifts to those who ask him! (Matthew 7:7-8,11).

Prayer enables us to know God and to ever receive his manifold provision like Aaron, Moses and Hur did. As those three men on the mountain prayed, the Amalekites found out they were not just fighting against the Israelites, but against the Lord God almighty!

As we pray to access the new covenant, we are praying in agreement with God's will. Jesus tells us in Matthew that if two or three on earth agree in prayer about anything, it will be done by the Father in heaven, because when we agree in prayer with other believers, he is in our midst. Agreement is covenant language. When you pray for your pastor, you are in agreement with the Father's will and desire.

Friendly fire, on the other hand, is disagreement. Criticism is out of sync with the Father's oneness in love and honor.

Prayer hedges make sense when you understand covenant commitment and relationship. The whole concept of covenant makes available to you the resources of God on behalf of your shepherd to equip him or her for the calling of ministry.

Access to the Covenant

One of my closest friends is the Reverend Gregg Parris, pastor of Union Chapel in Muncie, Indiana. In March, 1991 Gregg's wife was diagnosed with cancer. The prognosis was not good.

"It was a very stressful time in our lives," he said. Over a period of six months, Gregg's wife went through surgery, radiation and chemotherapy. There were some very dark days for the couple—times when the outcome could easily have gone one way or the other.

"I have known the blessing of being an intercessor for many people with life-threatening problems," the young pastor said. "However, this is the first time I encountered the profound and unmistakable benefits of the prayer covenant that Beth and I have with God."

For Gregg, nothing could have been more real. "It was the most amazing experience," he said. "Beth and I were buoyed up, sustained and protected by the grace of God that came to us through the intercessory prayers of our lay people."

The 37-year old pastor said that words cannot describe the peace of the Lord that he and his wife came to know. "Through the loving, fervent and sincere prayers of God's people, my wife and I discovered that the Lord can cause light to shine in the darkest of places," he said.

In the Bible, the name of God is the key to accessing the covenant in God's will and character. For example, Deuteronomy 12:5 states, "But you are to seek the place the LORD your God will choose from among all your tribes to put his Name there for his dwelling. To that place you must go . . ." His name in covenant represents his presence, his character, his holiness and his greatness. To take his name in vain is to miss this understanding.

In the Old Testament, seven covenant names were given to the people to access the covenant of provision in prayer. They are:

Jehovah—The Great I Am (Exodus 3:14)

Jehovah Jireh—The Provider (Genesis 22:14)

El Shaddai—The Lord God Almighty (Genesis 49:24-25)

Adonai—Our Shield (Genesis 15:1-3)

Jehovah Rophi—The Healer (Exodus 15:26)

Jehovah M Kadesh—The Righteous One (Leviticus 20:7-8)

Jehovah Nissi—Our Banner (Exodus 17:15)

To know God's name in covenant was to know him personally, and the blessing of the covenant was made available. As people called upon his name, they were blessed in right-standing, holiness, mercy and healing. This aspect of blessing was particularly strong in the Abrahamic covenant.

Today, when we pray in the name of Jesus, we are still blessed through God's covenant with Abraham. Through his blood, Christ transformed the old covenant into the new one, making all the same provisions available to us. Since the old covenant was secured through the blood of Jesus, it is through his name alone that we access the new covenant. Therefore, you can bless your pastor through prayer in Jesus' name. He said, "And I will do whatever you ask in my name, so that the Son may bring glory to the Father. You may ask me for anything in my name, and I

> *To pray in Jesus' name protects us from praying human-centered prayers.*

will do it" (John 14:13-14). Several times Jesus told us to pray in his name, and remembering the old covenant, his name represents his personhood, character and power.

To pray in Jesus' name protects us from praying human-centered prayers. Covenant prayer is not me getting my will done in heaven. It is agreeing with God and getting his will done on earth. Prayer in Jesus' name is not for improving my golf game or getting a parking space at the mall, it is praying in line with his desires and his holiness. For example, to pray in Jesus' name is to pray for healing, peace and salvation for the lost. It is to pray for the strength to overcome temptation and resist the devil and for the will to forgive and to reconcile. These are requests in line with the "anything" Jesus spoke of in John 14. God warns us against human-centered prayer, saying,

> You do not have, because you do not ask God. When you ask, you do not receive, because you ask with wrong motives, that you may spend what you get on your pleasures (James 4:2-3).

Covenant praying in Jesus' name is like the power of attorney—it means we have the power to act on earth in accordance with our God in heaven with whom we are "bonded." Jesus died on the cross, and was raised from the dead to take his seat in the heavenlies. He was the man who kept covenant with God so that we could pray and minister in his stead on the earth.

A prayer hedge in Jesus' name fully represents his will and interests in kingdom matters. For example, the enemy has a quiver full of darts of fear that he will use against a pastor—the fear of people and their opinions, the fear of opposition, the fear of taking a stand against abortion or racial injustice.

Fear is not of God. In Jesus' name, in accordance with his will, prayer warriors can bind and stand against fear aimed at a pastor. The personhood of Jesus and the finished work of Calvary stand as an ensign and force against the enemy's attempts to undermine a pastor's confidence with fear.

Praying in Jesus' name also protects and emboldens a pastor for Jesus. In Acts 4, Peter and John had been threatened not to preach in the name of Jesus. When the members of their prayer hedge met they prayed,

Now, Lord, consider their threats and enable your servants to speak your word
with great boldness. Stretch out your
hand to heal and perform miraculous
signs and wonders through the name of
your holy servant Jesus (Acts 4:29-30).

The answer was quick to come.

After they prayed, the place where they
were meeting was shaken. And they were
all filled with the Holy Spirit and spoke the
word of God boldly (Acts 4:31).

The force and power of a prayer hedge is in
the name of Jesus.

It is vital to understand that our prayers in
behalf of the pastor are not just to be spoken in
the name of Jesus, they are also heard in the
name of Jesus. God hears us based on the finished work of Jesus on the cross, not based on
our own holiness. Effective prayer is not just a
matter of duty, technique or volume. It is a matter of Jesus and his righteousness applied to our
petitions. A prayer hedge on behalf of a pastor
is effective because God answers based on the
covenant that was ratified by his son.

In light of this, why not pray for your pastor
right now, saying, "In Jesus' name I pray for
_____, that my God will count my
pastor worthy of his (or her) calling, and that by
his power, he may fulfill every good purpose of
my pastor and every act prompted by his (or her)
faith. I pray this so that the name of Jesus may
be glorified in my pastor according to the grace
of our God and the Lord Jesus Christ" (2
Thessalonians 1:11-12).

Praying the Word

In Jeremiah 1:12, the Lord says, "You have seen correctly, for I am watching to see that my word is fulfilled." In Psalms 145:18, David declares, "The Lord is near to all who call on him, to all who call on him in truth." Jesus said it this way:

> If you remain in me and my words remain in you, ask whatever you wish, and it will be given you. This is to my Father's glory, that you bear much fruit, showing yourselves to be my disciples (John 15:7-8).

As God gives us access to the new covenant in Jesus' name, he provides the vocabulary of covenant prayer in his Word. The covenant is based on God's faithful promises to his people, and our response to him is to keep his Word in our hearts. Deuteronomy 28:2,13 states,

> All these blessings will come upon you and accompany you if you obey the LORD your God....If you pay attention to the commands of the LORD your God that I give you this day and carefully follow them, you will always be at the top, never at the bottom.

The Lord told Joshua,

> Do not let this Book of the Law depart from your mouth; meditate on it day and night, so that you may be careful to do everything written in it. Then you will be prosperous and successful (Joshua 1:8).

God's commitment to us is his Word to us. So as covenant people, we take him based on his

Word. Therefore, when a prayer hedge prays for a pastor, the prayers should be rooted in scripture. Someone may ask, "What do I pray for in regard to my shepherd?" The answer is, "Pray what the Bible says for and about your pastor!" God's Word prayed for your pastor will not return void.

Reginald Klimionok calls praying the scriptures "truth praying." He writes, "Truth praying is a system of praying which encourages each Christian to pray out the great truths of God."[2]

The essence of truth praying is not to pray the problem or a need, but to lift to God what he has already promised in his Word. This kind of praying builds faith. For example, a group of men pray for me just before I preach. I kneel and they surround me. Based on Isaiah 50:4, one of them prays, "Lord, sovereign Lord, give my pastor an instructed tongue, let him know the word that sustains the weary. Morning by morning awaken Terry to your Word and teach him. Amen." Such encouragement causes my faith to soar as I get ready to go into the pulpit.

The Word is God's will for us, and we know that if we pray his will, he hears us and answers us (1 John 5:14-15). For example, the Bible teaches us that it is God's will for the lost to be saved. Proverbs 11:30 says "he who wins souls is wise." Thus, a prayer hedge could pray, "Lord, let my pastor be wise in soul winning and focused on seeking and winning the lost. Give my pastor your burden so that none shall perish. This is your will. So be it." In the same manner, you could pray for your pastor to heal the sick, which is also God's will. God is a promise-keeping God. Your pastor can see the sick healed and Jesus will be glorified.

In Ephesians 6, Paul lists the full armor of God as a source of protection and blessing. This is an excellent passage to pray over pastors to protect them as they do battle with the enemy! Remember, the forces of evil will use darts of skepticism, denial, disunity, seduction, coercion, disaster, depression and sickness against a pastor. The enemy is the antithesis of everything Jesus Christ stands for. Thank God for providing protection for pastors in the new covenant.

I have developed an entire prayer guide based on Ephesians 6 using the armor of God. This prayer guide comes with the manual, *Preyed On or Prayed For.* It focuses on the pastor's private life, personal or family life, his praise life, his prayer life, his professional life, preaching life and persevering life.

There are many examples of prayers based on the Word of God using Ephesians 6 as a starting point. For instance, in the section on claiming scriptural promises for overall protection is this prayer:

> Father, I thank you that no weapons formed against my shepherd will prosper. Every tongue raised against my leader will be cast down. Rumors and gossip will be turned aside. For Pastor _____ will be still before the Lord and will wait on you.
>
> My pastor will dwell in the shadow of the Most High God and will be delivered from terror, darts of doubt, and disease (Psalm 91:5-6). Let your angels guard my

pastor (Psalm 91:11) and no power of the
enemy shall harm _____ (Luke
10:19). Thank God forevermore!

Chapter 3 of this book contains 40 prayers
like this one based on scriptures to pray for your
pastor's protection and blessing.

An exciting benefit that comes from praying
scripture is that it is so rich in variety and creativity that prayer will not be repetitive, mundane
or boring. You can find countless passages in
addition to Ephesians 6 that can be prayed over
your pastor, such as Psalms 23. Can you imagine the power of a number of people speaking
this prayer for the pastor?

> The Lord is my pastor's shepherd; he (or
> she) will lack no good thing. You, Lord,
> give my pastor rest. Restore my pastor's
> energy. Guide my pastor in the paths of
> righteousness for your name's sake. Let
> no fear come near the parsonage. Comfort
> and anoint him (or her), and let my
> pastor's cup overflow! And Lord, as a
> church we are in agreement that goodness
> and mercy will follow our pastor every-
> where and he (or she) will richly dwell in
> your presence. Amen.

A scriptural focus like this brings the church
into a positive agreement concerning God's will
and intent for the shepherd of the flock. How
much better this is than "friendly fire!"

Covenant praying in the form of a prayer
hedge is based on God's Word to us in covenant.
When we pray the scriptures, we humbly remind
him what he has promised us, and in Jesus'

name we receive these promises based on what he did on the cross. Peter sums it up in 2 Peter 1:3-4:

> His divine power has given us everything we need for life and godliness through our knowledge of him who called us by his own glory and goodness. Through these he has given us his very great and precious promises, so that through them you may participate in the divine nature and escape the corruption in the world caused by evil desires.

The Holy Spirit and Prayer Hedges

One of the most powerful prayer hedges that ever met was in the Upper Room right after the Ascension.

In the first chapter of Acts, Jesus gave his disciples some final instructions. He told them not to leave Jerusalem but to wait for the Father to pour out the Holy Spirit upon them so that they would be empowered to witness. Then Jesus was taken up before their eyes to be with the Father. So the disciples returned to Jerusalem to the Upper Room to wait as Jesus had told them, and "to pray continually."

What happened next changed the course of history, and is still relevant today. In Acts 2, the Holy Spirit was poured out in a powerful manner just as Jesus had promised. Tongues of fire appeared on the pastors there, and they amazed the Jews in Jerusalem with their preaching. Pastor Peter reached out, and 3,000 souls were saved!

Prayer hedges invite the Holy Spirit to come and manifest the presence and power of God. What the early church pastors needed and received in this holy unction, contemporary pastors desperately need today. When you pray for your pastor, the Holy Spirit comes with new anointing. Even Jesus prayed to receive this anointing of the Holy Spirit during his ministry here on earth. In Luke 3:21, we read,

> When all the people were being baptized, Jesus was baptized too. And as he was praying, heaven was opened and the Holy Spirit descended on him in bodily form like a dove.

Again in Luke 5:16, we read, "But Jesus often withdrew to lonely places and prayed," and the next verse states, "And the power of the Lord was present for him to heal the sick." Later, Luke 6:12 says, "One of those days Jesus went out into the hills to pray, and spent the whole night praying to God." Then verse 19 says that people were trying to touch him "because power was coming from him and healing them all."

The Holy Spirit came to Jesus when he prayed, and likewise he will come to us when we pray. Even the very Son of God knew the importance of praying to invite the Spirit's anointing. He did not try to preach or heal without this power source. That is why, before the Ascension, he instructed his first pastors to stay in Jerusalem until they had been "clothed with power from on high." He knew they needed that power to spread the Gospel.

Jesus made it clear that the same power is available to us through prayer:

> If you then, though you are evil, know how to give good gifts to your children, how much more will your Father in heaven give the Holy Spirit to those who ask him! (Luke 11:13).

Prayer is a means of grace and anointing to equip us for the work of God. This was clearly seen in the book of Acts.

If anything is clear in the old covenant, it is this—God wanted people unto himself who were his own treasured possession. These people who bore his name and nature would be holy. They were to be so distinct that the other nations would take notice (Exodus 34:10). It would be impossible to hide the fact that these people were "bonded" to an almighty and everlasting God. His love for them would be very evident. They would be blessed in every way and they would be healthy (Deuteronomy 7:6-8, 13-15). They would know his glory and presence.

The outpouring of the Holy Spirit in Acts 2 amplified these intentions for the old covenant in the new covenant. The early church was the embodiment of all that the old covenant held to be true. But astoundingly, in the new covenant, the Holy Spirit would not just come upon a tent in the wilderness, or the Holy Place in the temple. He would fill every believer in Jesus! What an awesome thing!

This new creation would fan out from the Upper Room to manifest his presence in worship and demonstrate his greatness with signs and wonders. Prayer hedges would be planted and the fruits of the Spirit would begin to happen.

Pastors are blessed by the Holy Spirit as people pray. When we humble ourselves in prayer, we are emptied out, and like a wind, the Spirit rushes in and fills us with power for his work. The name and personhood of Jesus are exalted as a result of prayer hedges.

In Acts you will find 28 chapters with testimony after testi-

> *Riots could not stop them. Jails only made them pray and sing and win people to Christ.*

mony of the mighty acts of God in answer to prayer in the lives of pastors. Their preaching is powerful and fruitful. They heal the sick in Jesus' name. They meet opposition with an increased faith in God. These pastors had no books, tapes, or buildings. They were void of litanies and organization. Yet, they turned the world right-side up. When they had money, they gave it away. Their joy was contagious, and whole cities were infected by it. They did the works of God, casting out demons. They met racism head on and broke down its barriers. They ignited changed lives to spread the Gospel fire even further. Riots could not stop them. Jails only made them pray and sing and win people to Christ. Snake bites only set the stage for healing. Stonings did not keep them from preaching and shipwrecks could not deter them.

These pastors and apostles stayed on the crest of the Holy Spirit's impetus. They were untouchable with regard to sin and unstoppable with regard to obstacles. "The Lord's hand was with them, and a great number of people believed and turned to the Lord" (Acts 11:21). These New Testament pastors were the "point men" for a kingdom advance that hasn't concluded yet.

The State of the Church and its Effect on Pastors

This description of the church in Acts is a far cry from what many pastors today experience. Because of a lack of prayer hedges today, we view a church that on many fronts has not only conceded to retreat, it is actually scattering in full blown defeat!

The state of the church today is drastically affecting the well-being of pastors, and calls for an even more urgent mandate for prayer. Many conditions are taking a heavy toll on our leaders, seven of which I want to mention here. If ever we needed a fresh anointing of the Holy Spirit on shepherds, it is now!

1. A decline in membership

Recently *Newsweek* carried an article entitled, "Dead End for the Mainline?" which outlined the membership decline of some mainline denominations. According to their survey, the United Methodists have gone from 11.0 million members in 1965, to 8.7 million as of 1992. In most communities the average unchurched population represents between 67% and 70%. Yet, in these same cities, mainline churches are declining.[3]

I spoke recently to United Methodist pastors in Vermont, and I mentioned the term "profession of faith." One pastor raised his hand and asked, "What is a profession of faith? We haven't seen one in 20 years!" Pastors who don't see genuine conversions fight off depression. In my own conference, 40 percent of our churches do not show one single profession of faith in an entire year. That represents over 12,000 worship services without one person receiving salvation.

2. Lame worship

Worship in many churches today is boring. The music hasn't changed for 100 years, the litany for 200. The manifest presence of God is missing. The choir sings while the people watch. Unexciting worship such as this benefits only those who, through the years, have grown accustomed to it. Pastors suffer the most "doing" services where the presence of God is not experienced.

Worship is particularly unappealing to young people today. I heard a motivational speaker claim that in 1970, teens felt that the church was the number one influence in their lives growing up. By 1980, it had dropped to number four. And in 1990, teens didn't even mention the church as an influence. I believe there are fewer teens in the church now than ever in our history.

3. An absence of the Holy Spirit

The supernatural acts of the Holy Spirit, such as healing and deliverance, are often missing. We are ineffective when it comes to helping a society that is unraveling at the edges. We meet people with problems, and instead of being able to help, we simply act as a referral service. We plan weddings and conduct marriages, but we are unable to stem the tide of divorce right in our own families.

We are a church caught up in the natural, rationalistic, western view. Our loss of supernatural power leaves us limp in trying to stop abortion, domestic violence, teenage violence and child pornography.

We are so tame that people pass by our buildings on Sunday mornings without so much as a thought about what we are doing inside. I heard recently that a survey found that the church wasn't even ranked as one of the top twenty influences on society as a whole! Pastors in a non-worshipping community feel tired rather than inspired.

4. Reliance on marketing techniques

Many churches have resorted to the latest marketing techniques to get a crowd. One church growth book after another simply states, "Find their need and meet it, and you will attract people." We offer thousands of programs and gimmicks to try and increase our membership, often at the expense of true teaching and discipleship.

The sad result of this kind of approach is that we become very human-centered in all we do just to please people who might join. A human-centered gospel leaves out one important aspect—we the church are here to glorify God, not man. We have sold our bullets to buy a gun.

Pastors lose sight of their calling to confront sin when they try to make people "feel good" about themselves. Pastors lose identity when they sell out to marketing skills rather than the Holy Spirit's leading and vision implantation.

5. Division among churches

The church today is divided. Racism and denominationalism have taken their tolls. We conduct our services, but we are unable to conduct a city-wide prayer service because of unwillingness to put aside minor differences and work together. We are not one in purpose and too often our goal is to build up our own camps with certificates of transfer. Pastors caught in parochial promotion often become the "kept-men" of an institution that exists for its tradition and name pride. The only motivation they have left are their pension programs.

6. Moral decline

The church as a whole is at a moral low. The divorce rate of people in the church is no lower than the divorce rate of those on the outside. Holiness has given way to blessing "alternative life-styles." The hot issue for some church ruling bodies is the ordination of homosexuals rather than holiness as defined by the Bible.

When holiness and its definition are up for grabs, pastors lose their cutting edge. Fearful of being labeled "insensitive," they begin to tiptoe around issues lest they offend.

One of the most tragic pastoral falls of our era involves the sexual abuse of children by Catholic priests. According to *Newsweek*, the molestation of children is "the worst clerical scandal in the modern history of the U.S. Catholic Church." The article states that allegations have been brought against approximately 400 priests since 1982, and that probably 2,500 other cases have gone unreported. To make the situation worse, the church was "slow to recognize the seriousness of its problem," at times even went to great lengths to downplay or cover up the incidents.[4] When such tragedies make headlines, all churches share in the embarrassment. Pastors can get in serious trouble without prayerful accountability.

7. Prayerlessness

Prayerlessness is a characteristic of many churches today. Many churches have no payer room, no prayer coordinator, no prayer meetings, little prayer for the city and little or no prayer for the pastor. A prayerless church is like a sailboat without sails. The Spirit's wind may be blowing, but there are no sails to catch it.

Pastoring a prayerless church causes a pastor to depend on money and manpower to get the job done—neither of which are very effective in the spiritual realm. Many pastors become like hummingbirds, skipping from one promotional project to another in a frenzied excitement that would leave a high school cheerleader exhausted!

Museum Duty

Do some experiences give you an eerie feeling?

Recently, my wife and I toured the U.S.S. Lexington. Now in permanent dock in Corpus

Christi, Texas, for a half-century this mammoth aircraft carrier saw more action than any other American warship. Today it's a floating museum of war relics!

The youthful crew, few of whom have ever seen combat, simply show photos and movies of the once-proud ship's "glory days" to hundreds of tourists who tromp up and down its steel-plated decks each day. The war planes are bolted down, never to fly again. The combat information room is silent. Places that not long ago hummed with the activity of thousands of young men in full battle alert are now deadly still. A heavily armored room that formerly served as the storehouse for tons of ammunition is now a tastefully decorated coffee shop. The crew of the Lexington still looks polished and ready for battle, but their only responsibilities now are to give tours, pour coffee and entertain people with stories of past exploits.

As I stood on the upper deck, my hands grasping the rail, my heart swelled with the realization that the fate of our country once rested in this and a half-dozen other carriers. And, as I turned to leave, I felt a ghostly sense of sadness as I viewed this once powerful, proud, military vessel that had become a place for gawking tourists.

As we were being led through the tour, I thought of many pastors today who are much like the present crew of the Lexington—pastors who hold up pictures of past captains and tell of their missions, pastors who show the war reels of victory only to see defeat in the eyes of their parishioners, pastors today who simulate something that is unreal and irrelevant to families being torn apart by moral failures and pastors who get the mail, order the candles, mow the grass and try to keep everybody happy.

Isn't it enough to make you cry! How sad it is that these modern day pastors have been taken off the front lines, stripped of the supernatural, toned down and left with little passion for lost souls. How sad it is to see pastors using modern marketing techniques to get the crowd in for a head count. How tragic is the identity crisis in preaching as revealed by pastors who flip through the latest book looking for a sermon.

> *Pastors are frustrated because they signed up to serve on a battleship, but got museum duty instead!*

No wonder pastors are burned out! They are tired of talking about what was and only imagining what could be. Pastors are frustrated because they signed up to serve on a battleship, but got museum duty instead! Many pastors would love to turn things around, but their efforts are useless without the support of the laity.

A few years ago I preached at a church in New York. As I spoke, I noticed that the organist was reading a magazine! During my entire sermon, I never once saw her look up. I later found out that she had become angry because of some changes that had taken place in the church and her method of retaliation was to ignore anyone who set foot in the pulpit! The most tragic thing about the situation was that the laity wouldn't support the pastor's efforts to remove her.

Because of the church's state of affairs, many pastors are taking it on the chin. Like the coach of an 0-10 team, the pastor gets the blame for the losses. No wonder hundreds of pastors are discarded every month because they don't produce. In some respects, the church has had too many losing seasons in a row!

Pastors are hard pressed. Instead of managing revival, they often spend valuable time managing the flock's divorces and petty complaints. Anyone who has been pastoring for several years has probably had plenty of visits or phone calls from angry members saying, "I wanted to sing the solo this morning" or "You misspelled my name in the bulletin" or "My daughter didn't get a part in the Christmas play!" My favorite was, "You didn't pray with me this morning at the altar. Why don't you like me?" The pastor of an East Texas church felt led to let a teen lead the praise service one Sunday night. The official song leader got so angry because he hadn't been consulted first that he left the church. The pastor had to beg him to come back.

It is little wonder that pastors retire on the inside at 35 and jump overboard in affairs and moral crises. These placidly predictable preachers are a sad contrast to their predecessors in the book of Acts. The call to pray for our pastors in a new and bold manner is urgent if we are to break out of the cocoon of religious doldrums.

One denomination has a room with files stacked to the ceiling of defrocked ministers. I talked to the secretary of that room who handles ministerial credentials, and he just wept as he told me of the most recent file added—his own pastor.

As we look at the current state of affairs, we can hear the Lord's plea in Ezekiel 22:30,

> I looked for a man among them who would build up the wall and stand before me in the gap on behalf of the land so I would not have to destroy it, but I found none.

Will the Lord find any to stand in the gap and restore the prayer hedge for shepherds today?

Much more is in jeopardy than just the personal lives of pastors and their marriages. The future of the church in America is at stake. The church's ability to be that redemptive, powerful, chosen nation of God to proclaim Jesus Christ to every nation is on the line.

We are like a great warship, sailing into enemy waters to free the captives and undo the works of Satan. We need pastors who are fully alive in Christ to lead the way. If there is no fire in the pulpit, there will be no fire in the pew. If the pastor has no vision, board meetings will be visionless and boring as well. If the pastor does not have a passion for lost souls, certainly the laity won't either. The church may have a board of elders, but there must be a leader among leaders to set the pace and sound the trumpet.

Every year at our annual conference, I am deeply troubled by what I see in the book room. Worn out, overweight ministers circle the book table thinking, "Maybe this new book on church growth will be the answer. If I can just find out about the latest techniques, I'm sure my church will flourish!" Unfortunately, this approach has not worked in 20 years.

What we really need is a new and fresh outpouring of the Holy Spirit, not just a new technique. I'm not speaking of a denominational version of revival, or a short term flurry of excitement and emotionalism. Nor am I speaking of the "charismatic movement," but rather THE charismatic impetus of Acts 1-28. We need a baptism of the Spirit to anoint and empower pastors to enter into a whole new dimension of preaching and leading! I believe the hope for this divine outpouring will be prayer hedges beseeching God in behalf of their pastors.

Will you stand in the gap and pray? If so, let me suggest a way to pray for your pastor and even the other pastors of your city. The book of Acts has 28 chapters, just enough to read and pray one chapter a day for a month. At the end of the year, you will have prayed the book of Acts twelve times over your pastor. Just think of the difference that will make in your pastor's life and ministry!

An interesting thing to note about Acts is that it appears to be unfinished. The last chapter concludes with, "Boldly and without hindrance he [Paul] preached the kingdom of God and taught about the Lord Jesus Christ." Acts has no personal remarks to anyone at the end (as it does at the beginning) or any formal closure like the other books in the New Testament such as, "The grace of the Lord Jesus be with you." I think this is because Acts, the acts of the Holy Spirit, are not finished. The Holy Spirit is still expanding the church as he did in chapters 1-28. What he did back then he still wants to do today. We have a blueprint of what we are to do and build. In fact, every church has a commission to write chapter 29 right where they are, be it Corbin, Kentucky; Orlando, Florida; or Snook, Texas.

> *With your Bible open to Acts in one hand and a picture of your pastor in the other, you can pray, "Holy Spirit, in Jesus' name, do it again!"*

The first 28 chapters reveal a prototype of what God intended the church to become, but it is up to us to continue the story. With your Bible open to Acts in one hand and a picture of your pastor in the other, you can pray, "Holy Spirit, in Jesus' name, do it again!"

Starting in Acts 1, you could pray, "Call us to an Upper Room to pray continually. Build in us a launching pad to send our pastor out to preach with apostolic results."

From Acts 2, you can pray, "Let my pastor preach like Peter did. Let my pastor be filled with the Spirit to preach, and let us say, 'What must we do to be saved?' Let us repent and turn to Jesus Christ completely."

You can pray from Acts 3, "Reveal the power of Jesus' name to my shepherd. May he (or she) heal the sick and glorify Jesus as the Healer."

Acts 4 teaches us to pray, "Lord, let us lift our pastor's hands to face opposition and resistance to the Gospel. Form us into a prayer hedge to pray. Consider the threats against our pastor and enable your servant to speak your Word with great boldness. Stretch out your hand to heal and perform miraculous signs and wonders through the name of your holy servant Jesus."

Pray from Acts 5, "Lord, expose compromise and sin. Let my pastor be like Peter in confronting the spirit of Ananias and Sapphira in our city and let my pastor's message bring healing to families."

From Acts 6, pray, "Let my minister prioritize his or her time to be devoted to prayer and the ministry of the Word. Deliver my pastor from "busyness" and the urgency of nonessentials."

These are just a few sample prayers taken from the rich source of material found in Acts that you can pray for your local church pastor. Pray that your pastor will be like Philip in chapter eight. Give your pastor, through prayer, Damascus Road conversions as in chapter nine.

Acts 10 is great for prayer to gain spiritual breakthroughs in dealing with racism. You can use chapter 12 to pray for the pastors of your city who are in prisons of discouragement and public opinion. Ask God to send angels to free them as they did Peter.

What pastors need today is a fresh outpouring of the Holy Spirit. As you form a prayer hedge, you will see it happen!

Fifty Ways to Promote Prayer for Pastors

1. Calvary Assembly Church in Orlando picks one pastor and one church per week to pray over in their Sunday morning service. You may want to put the names of the church and pastor in the bulletin under pastoral prayer. Calvary notifies the pastors and churches that they pray for. This is good modeling to promote unity and support to churches and pastors.

2. Churches in a District or Association can exchange the names of pastors and pray for God's protection and blessing on those pastors. These prayer assignments can be made for specific periods of time such as ninety days or less. It is important to share answers

to these prayers to promote praise and continued prayer.

3. The men's group of the local church can pray for the pastor. The men in the Aldersgate United Methodist Church meet at 8:00 a.m. on Sundays to pray for the pastoral staff. This is also the case in Dr. John Maxwell's church, Skyline Wesleyan, and in Dr. Mark Rutland's church, Calvary Assembly.

4. If your church has a prayer room, you can put a picture of the pastor in it to remind people to pray. Church on the Rock in Rockwall, Texas, has a prayer station with pictures of the pastor and staff members, and their ministries listed for prayer. As people sign up to pray, the pastor will be prayed for daily. In one church, the pastor leaves a tape in the prayer room every week telling the prayer room warriors how to pray for him.

5. Ask your church board to budget an annual prayer retreat for the pastor. There are numerous such retreats being raised up around the country. Give your pastor the church's blessing and financial support to go. Successful pastors believe it is important to take such retreats to help them focus on and listen to God's voice.

6. In every local church, there are people who own lake cabins or maintain retreat houses. Maybe they will be willing to allow your pastor to use such places to get away and seek

God. Try to find a place of retreat for your pastor. I draw apart one day each week for prayer and meditation. I've done this for the past thirteen years and I can testify that it has made all the difference in my life and ministry. Therefore, I am intentional in finding a place to be alone with God. My church gives me their blessing in this practice.

7. Place the names of your Bishop, District Superintendent or denominational leader in the church bulletin every week for prayer. By honoring your leaders, you honor God's authority and order for the local church. As mentioned earlier, the Pope and local Bishop are prayed for in every mass conducted in the Catholic Church.

8. Solicit the local church's women's group to pray for the pastor and his or her family. Share this book and the manual *Preyed On or Prayed For* with them to promote creative ways of praying for your shepherd. This special emphasis could run six weeks or more.

9. The pastor of South Oaks Baptist Church has 27 men signed up to pray for him. On Mondays he meets for breakfast with the week's seven and tells them how to pray for him in the coming week. For example, Sam is to pray on Tuesday, the pastor's counseling day, so he can pray for wisdom. Thursday is sermon preparation day, so Frank's assignment is to pray for rich study time and no distractions. This approach helps the men bond with the pastor and lets them know what is going on in his life.

10. Encourage your pastor to pray with other pastors. A group of pastors meets weekly in Austin to pray for the city and each other. They meet on the top floor of a downtown hotel so that they have a good view to inspire specific prayer over sections of the city. Interdenominational pastors' prayer groups are springing up everywhere.

> *Encourage your pastor to pray with other pastors.*

11. Adult Sunday school classes can pray for the pastor on Sunday. The Sunday school superintendent could distribute copies of your pastor's preaching text for the classes to pray over. They can pray that the Word would go forth with power and authority.

12. If the church has cell groups, they can be involved in praying for the pastor. This could work on a rotational basis by passing the pastor's prayer portfolio from group to group. A group meeting in a home could pray for a month and then pass on the prayer privilege.

    This prayer portfolio would include the pastor's vision for the church. It would also have any expressed needs that the pastor feels in his or her life. It might also contain your pastor's schedule and sermon text for the next few weeks. This portfolio should be well thought out and well presented because so much depends on it.

13. Involve the church youth group in praying for the pastor. With appropriate prayer guides, the youth can be a mighty hedge for your shepherd.

14. Sunday morning worship offers a good opportunity to pray for your shepherd. A lay leader could be designated to read the text and then pray for the pastor's life and sermon. This idea is good because it models prayer for the pastor in front of the entire congregation. Sometimes prayer is better caught than taught.

15. Use this book and the manual *Preyed On or Prayed For* as a six-week teaching curriculum for teaching people how to pray for their leader. The class could even write their own prayer guide and personalize it to their pastor's specific needs.

16. Church members could be asked to write prayers based on the Scriptures and then mail them to their pastor. These prayer letters could be a source of encouragement to the pastor. Plus, they promote good prayer habits for leadership.

17. The sanctuary of the local church could be opened early prior to services to invite people to pray for the pastor and the services. The members would simply sit in the sanctuary an hour early to pray quietly for the pastor to be blessed in presenting the Gospel.

18. Make a list of the pastors and churches in the city available for specific prayer. We have a list of churches in our prayer room.

19. Conduct a 24-hour prayer vigil four times a year. Have people sign up to come on Saturday for one hour time slots to intercede for the shepherd. Give them a prayer guide and thank them for caring enough to pray. These vigils would coincide with Easter or other crucially important Sundays.

20. Lead a prayer group to pray through the book of Acts for your pastor. You could use the *Acts 29 Prayer Resource.*[1] Simply ask the Father to do in your pastor's life what was done in the book of Acts. This would take 50 days.

21. Ask the youth group to baby-sit the pastor's children free so the pastor and his or her spouse can be alone with God.

22. If your church has a church staff, promote prayer for each staff member using the practical ideas above. Encourage the staff to pray for each other and to have corporate prayer time.

23. Teach the members of your church to pray over the pastor and his or her family when they have their evening meal. Ask the Lord to bless your pastor, his or her spouse and children. Omar Cabrera of Argentina has mobilized his congregation of 90,000 to pray for him each time their families sit down to a meal. Imagine the power of this even if only a fourth remember to pray for him each day.

24. Encourage the choir to pray for the pastor during the sermon. Teach them to pray short prayers like, "Help our pastor, Lord,"

and, "Holy Spirit quicken our pastor during the invitation." As your pastor preaches, the choir can also pick out a face in the congregation and pray for that person to receive the message. If someone looks distressed, focus on that person to be comforted and built up. The choir can be a great source of prayer backing up the minister. The pastor could even tell them his or her requests.

25. Stress the importance of "pew-praying" for the pastor. As people come in, they can say a short prayer for their pastor. During the service they can pray—especially during the invitation.

26. Ask the ushers to pray for your pastor as they present the offering. Prayer modeling facilitates congregational praying for leaders.

27. At Central Baptist Church in Bryan, Texas, the deacons take time to pray on their knees while Pastor Chris is preaching. This church has two morning services and one evening service and they have 100 deacons who share in this ministry. This special group of intercessors is called "The Watchmen."

28. Remind your Administrative Board to pray for the minister. The Board may assign this prayer task each meeting to a different leader who can then prepare a prayer for the pastor.

29. In most churches, members are expected to have a devotional time every day. For most Christians, this is a perpetual goal as well as a time of personal growth. Simply ask

them to include their pastor in their personal prayer time each day.

30. Publish the pastor's vision so members can pray for it to come to pass. Make it succinct and to the point. Put it on a card so people can keep it in their Bible for easy reference and lift it up often.

31. Use routinely published material in the church such as newsletters, bulletins or reports to remind people to pray for their shepherd. A simple phrase at the bottom like "Remember to pray for the pastor" is all it takes.

32. Once a year, bring your pastor and his or her family to the altar to lay hands on them and renew the church's commitment to pray for them. This helps to visually communicate to the congregation both the need for prayer and the privilege that it is to be able to lift up the pastor. The Morning Star Baptist Church is a small church, yet once a year they have a pastor's appreciation day. At the close of the service they put two chairs in front for the pastor and his or her spouse and ask people to come one at a time to pray for them.

33. Print Bible book markers with the church's denominational leadership listed along with local church staff so people can pray for these individuals by name.

34. Use the church newsletter to incite prayer for your pastor. Print your pastor's schedule to promote daily prayer for the Lord to

bless him or her. Use one-liners like "Remember to pray for the pastor" or "Keep your shield over our minister" or "Let's claim Philippians 4:19 for our shepherd this week."

35. Print some bumper stickers that read, "Have you prayed for your pastor today?" This elevates community awareness to pray for all pastors.

> *Print some bumper stickers that read, "Have you prayed for your pastor today?"*

36. Remind your pastor to inform the church when he or she has a funeral so people can pray at the exact hour your pastor stands up to comfort the family.

37. Talk to your District Superintendent or Area Association about praying for pastors at the District monthly preacher's meeting. Encourage them to come forward and put their hands on the pastors and pray that they be healed and renewed.

    One denominational leader of the Church of God in Cleveland, Tennessee has a unique way of praying for pastors. He calls them together with their spouses. Usually, this is a gathering of 10 or 20 persons. He then ministers to them by serving communion to them. He places a wooden cross on the floor along with pieces of paper, nails and a hammer. As he speaks of hurts and difficulties in ministry, he encourages the pastors to forgive the people who have hurt them. He asks them to write the names on the paper and nail them to the cross. Then he takes the papers off the cross and he burns them right there in front of them. He prays for them during this whole time. This is a unique and wonderful way to minister to leaders.

38. This same church collects names of pastors, spouses and children and gives this list to all their retirees to pray over in a ministry called "Prayer Bound." The Church of God pastors are very encouraged when they discover their denomination is prayerfully concerned about them and their children.

> *During the day, people can call the church and find out how to pray for their pastor.*

39. Write your area Overseer, Bishop or Devotional President to have all the pastors come forward at the annual meeting for prayer and personal ministry. On the day of this special prayer, notify the churches to pray.

40. One pastor set up a telephone answering service, and on the recordings he gave a list of things his members could pray about for him. During the day, people can call the church and find out how to pray for their pastor.

41. Call the Oral Roberts Prayer Tower (918/495-7777) and ask them to pray for your pastor to be a great soul winner.

42. Make place cards for your table that read: "Have you prayed for your pastor today?"

43. Circulate a list of local prison chaplains so they can be prayed for. Pastors who have no church desperately need prayer.

44. Write to the Upper Room in Nashville, Tennessee, and include a brief prayer list for your pastor to be lifted up. Their address is 1908 Grand Avenue, P. O. Box 189, Nashville, Tennessee, 37202-0189, ATTN.: Prayer Room.

45. Use objects and sites to remind people in the church to pray at random. For example, teach your fellow members that every time they pass a church, they could say a short prayer for their own shepherd. If your pastor likes golf, they can put a golf ball in their car and pray for their pastor every time they touch the ball or drive by a golf course.

46. Use church bulletin boards to remind people to pray for the staff or pastor. The artist in the church could create beautiful ways to spark prayer for the shepherd.

47. On the National Day of Prayer in May gather at pulpits in your area to pray for pastors that they will bring a strong message of revival and holiness in the land.

48. Buy several copies of this book and the companion manual *Preyed On or Prayed For* and lay them around the church, or circulate them among the leadership.

49. Start an "Aaron and Hur Society" to lift up

the pastor's hands and promote camaraderie in praying for the shepherd.

50. Simply and spontaneously thank God for your pastor often because he or she is a special gift from God to you and your church.

Twelve Guidelines for Prayer for Pastors

Cindy Jacobs offers the following advice to people she calls prayer partners who are praying for their shepherd. Her suggestions apply to both close, personal partners as well as intercessors who may be part of a large team.[1]

1. Come as a servant to the leaders. Realize that they are not there to meet your needs and the prayer needs of your family. Although they pray for their partners, do not take advantage of them. They will appreciate that quality in you since most people usually want only to take from them. Rarely are they on the receiving end.

2. When you talk to them on the phone, state what the Lord has given you quickly and

concisely. They are often extremely busy people and may feel obligated to talk even though it will cause them to be pressed for time the rest of the day. A good idea is to ask if they are busy or if it would be better to call at a different time.

If you have a dream or vision, ask the Lord for interpretation.

3. Don't be offended if they don't speak to you in person. They may or may not be able to do so at that moment. This does not mean they don't care.

4. Be careful not to overload emotionally the person for whom you are praying. If you have a heavy warning from God for them, be sensitive as to whether or not they can handle hearing the warning without being overwhelmed.

5. If you have a dream or vision, ask the Lord for interpretation. It is your job to interpret, not theirs. If you are not sure that something you are receiving is from the Lord, take more time to pray.

6. It may take time to build trust in the validity of your ministry of intercession. Be faithful in your praying and the relationship will come.

7. Do not presume upon your relationship with Christian leaders. They will treasure you both as an intercessor and as a person if you don't tell personal details or flaunt the

fact that you are their prayer partner. This is a confidential trust.

8. Remember to pray for the families of the leaders. This is critical because they come under strong attack from the enemy as well.

9. The Lord may give you a focus of prayer. In other words, you may be a "specialist" in certain areas. I have found that some of my partners pray pretty much exclusively for my children. They tell me, "I pray very little for you as a minister." Others will pray for my husband more than they pray for me. Some will pray for me to be free from any moral temptations.

10. Give leaders feedback on a regular basis on what the Lord is telling you. Either call or write at least every few months.

11. There are two times when ministers for whom you intercede are especially needy: the night before they minister and the time directly after.

    The night before they minister is often a time when family members get harassed and many distractions come to divide the mind of the leader from preparing for the time of ministry. Things break down; strife tries to enter; children come under oppression. Just like Jesus in the Garden, the leader for whom you pray would welcome prayer during the Gethsemane time.

    The time when the minister has finished the assignment is also particularly vulnerable. For pastors this is usually the Monday after a Sunday of spiritual breakthrough. Many have told me how depression will try to hit. This is often the time when people express criticism of the pastor. Leaders are vulnerable to criticism of the pastor. Leaders are vulnerable to criticism right after they have ministered extensively and exhaustively. Satan knows this. Notice that the angels came and ministered to Jesus after His time in the wilderness.

For some reason it seems that most traveling ministers experience warfare for nearly two weeks after they come home from a prolonged trip. Sometimes it is a physical attack, sometimes financial. It often occurs when they are exhausted and are most in need of a time of refreshing. Prayer partners should not stop praying for the leaders until the Lord gives them a release that all is well on the home front. This will stop or lessen the backlash from the enemy.

12. As a prayer partner, pray for protection for your own family as you intercede. I suggest that you read Psalm 91 out loud daily.

Notes

Notes

Chapter One

1 Joe Aldrich shared this disturbing statistic with a group of pastors in Atlanta.

Chapter Two

1 C. Peter Wagner, *Prayer Shield* (Ventura, CA: Regal Books), 1992, p. 63.

2 George Barna, *Today's Pastors* (Ventura, CA: Regal Books), 1993, pp. 61-62.

3 Adapted from George Barna, *Today's Pastors*, 1993, p. 52.

4 C. Peter Wagner, *Prayer Shield*, pp. 78-79.

5 Adapted from George Barna, *Today's Pastors*, 1993, p. 52.

6 George Barna, *Today's Pastors*, pp. 63-65, 130.

7 Ralph W. Neighbour, Jr., *Where Do We Go From Here?* (Houston: Touch Publications), 1990, p. 19.

8 E. M. Bounds, *The Complete Works of E. M. Bounds on Prayer* (Grand Rapids: Baker Book House), 1990, p. 486.

Chapter Three

1 Dick Eastman, *The Hour That Changes the World* (Grand Rapids: Baker Book House), 1992.

2 Cindy Jacobs, *Possessing the Gates of the Enemy* (Grand Rapids: Baker Book House), 1993, p. 163.

3 C. Peter Wagner, *Prayer Shield*, pp. 182-183.

4 C. Peter Wagner, *Prayer Shield*, pp. 104-116.

5 C. Peter Wagner, *Prayer Shield*, p. 109.

6 George Barna, *Today's Pastors*, p. 145.

7 C. Peter Wagner, *Prayer Shield*, p. 115.

8 George Barna, *Today's Pastors*, p. 40.

Chapter Four

1 Paul Y. Cho, *Prayer: Key to Revival* (Dallas: Word Publishing), 1984.

2 Charles Stanley, *How to Start a Prayer Group and Keep It Growing* (Atlanta: First Baptist Church of Atlanta), 1980.

Chapter Five

1 Dudley Hall, *Out of the Comfort Zone* (Pineville, NC: Morning Star), 1991.

2 C. Peter Wagner, *Warfare Prayer* (Ventura, CA: Regal Books), 1982, p. 61.

3 Terry Teykl, *Making Room to Pray*

4 Richard Hammar, "Pastors, Seduction and the Law," *Ministries Today,* July/August 1993, p. 36.

5 C. Peter Wagner, *Prayer Shield,* p. 66.

6 C. Peter Wagner, *Prayer Shield,* p. 66.

Chapter Six

1 C. Peter Wagner, *Prayer Shield,* p. 182-183.

2 Reginald Klimionok, *How to Put on God's Armour* (Franklin Springs, GA: Advocate Press), 1988, p. 26.

3 Kenneth L. Woodward, "Dead End for the Mainline?" *Newsweek,* August 9, 1993, pp. 46-47.

4 "Priests and Abuse," *Newsweek,* August 16, 1993, pp. 42-44.

Appendix A

1 Terry Teykl, *Acts 29 Prayer Resource*

Appendix B

1 Cindy Jacobs, *Possessing the Gates of the Enemy,* pp. 168-171.